BreakInG CHaInS:

The New Underground Railroad

Steve Taylor

Copyright © 2023 by Steve Taylor

All rights reserved.

Copyright Notice and Disclaimer

©Steve Taylor, [2023]. All Rights Reserved.

The content provided herein, including texts, graphics, images, and other material, is for informational purposes only and is the exclusive property of [Steve Taylor]. This content is protected under applicable copyright laws and international treaties. No part of this material may be reproduced, distributed, transmitted, displayed, published, or broadcast without the prior written permission of Steve Taylor, except as provided for by the terms of fair use under copyright law.

This material is provided "as is" without warranty of any kind, either express or implied, including but not limited to implied warranties of merchantability, fitness for a particular purpose, or non-infringement. References to other works, publications, or sources of material within this content are provided for informational purposes only and do not imply endorsement or approval of the referenced content.

Steve Taylor does not claim ownership of any copyrighted material other than its own. The use of any such material is intended for educational, or informational purposes and is believed to be in fair use. Any use of copyrighted material that is not in accordance

BREAKING CHAINS:

with fair use or other copyright exceptions is prohibited and will be rectified promptly upon notification.

This notice does not constitute legal advice. If you require legal advice regarding copyright or other legal matters, please consult a qualified attorney.

By using this content, you agree to indemnify and hold harmless Steve Taylor and STCNC publishing from and against any claims, liabilities, damages, losses, or expenses, including reasonable attorneys' fees and costs, arising out of or in any way connected with your access to or use of this content.

This copyright notice is subject to change without notice.

CONTENTS

Best
Sellers

The Chronicles of Mary
Magdelene Series

Mary's Salvation
The Illuminated Path
Jerusalem's Faith
Paul's Odyssey
Andrew's Adventures
Mary's Celestial Journey
In the Company
of Angels
John's Journey
Heaven's Warriors
Isabella's Divine Destiny

Steve Taylor
Https://maryschronicles.online

"Breaking Chains

"Breaking Chains: The New Underground Railroad" explores the biblical teachings on human dignity and the abolition of modern slavery. This book is designed to help readers gain a deeper understanding of the Christian perspective on this issue and to provide practical tools for action. Whether you are a Christian leader, an activist, or simply someone who cares about justice, this book will equip you to make a difference in the fight against modern slavery. As Christians, we are called to be agents of change in the world, to bring light to the darkness and hope to the hopeless. We are to be a force for good in the world, to seek justice and defend the oppressed. And one of the most pressing challenges of our time is the issue of modern-day slavery. Yes, slavery still exists in our world today, and it's time for us to take action and unchain those who are still in bondage.

But where do we begin? How can we as Christians lead the charge against slavery? First, we must recognize the reality of the situation. Despite being illegal in every country, slavery still exists in various forms around the world, from forced labor to sex trafficking. It's a global issue that demands a global response. Second, we need to educate ourselves and others about the issue. We need to understand the root causes of slavery, such as poverty, lack of education, and corruption, and work to address those underlying issues. We also need to recognize the signs of slavery and trafficking and know how to report them to the authorities.

Third, we need to support organizations that are working to combat slavery and provide assistance to survivors. This includes organizations that provide shelter, counseling, job training, and legal services to those who have been freed from slavery. But perhaps most importantly, we need to approach this issue with a mindset of love and compassion. We need to see those who are enslaved not as statistics or problems to be solved, but as fellow human beings created in the image of God. We need to walk alongside them, listen to their stories, and provide support and encouragement as they begin their journey towards freedom and healing.

In short, we as Christians have a unique opportunity and responsibility to lead the charge against slavery. Let's commit ourselves to this cause, to unchaining those who are still in bondage, and to bringing hope and freedom to the world.

"UNCHAINED: HOW CHRISTIANS CAN LEAD THE CHARGE AGAINST SLAVERY"

The night was shrouded in darkness, its secrets hidden within the dancing shadows. With each passing moment, an unspoken tension filled the air, leaving behind a trail of unanswered questions and an impending sense of peril. Unbeknownst to them, their lives were on the brink of an irreversible transformation, all sparked by a single, fateful encounter.

In a world where chains bind the souls of the oppressed, a guide emerges. "Breaking Chains: delves into the depths of human dignity and the fight against modern slavery. This epic tale takes readers on a journey through the annals of time, exploring the teachings of ancient wisdom and the quest for liberation. It is a guide that transcends boundaries, offering practical tools and insights to those who seek to make a difference.

Within these pages, the essence of a Christian perspective unfolds, illuminating the path towards justice and freedom. Leaders, activists, and compassionate souls alike will find solace in its words, as they become equipped to combat the darkness that plagues our world. For it is our divine calling to be catalysts of change, to bring hope to the hopeless and light to the shadows. In the veiled corners of our modern world, where the sinister echoes of an age-old evil still reverberate, a new saga unfolds. It's a narrative drenched in the grim realities of modern slavery – forced labor, human trafficking, and debt bondage – forms of oppression that defy the very essence of human dignity. This story, deeply rooted in the righteous crusade of historical abolitionists, is a relentless pursuit of freedom in the face of contemporary darkness.

As the night cloaks the city streets, a hushed gathering of dedicated souls convenes in a dimly lit hall. They are the modern-day abolitionists, a diverse coalition bound by a shared mission – to eradicate the malignant growth of slavery that still festers in the shadows of society. Among them is Sarah, a fervent advocate whose spirit is ignited by the teachings of 1 John 4:20 and Galatians 3:28. She, like her fellow warriors, is driven by a profound Christian ethos that recognizes no boundary in race or gender, seeing all as equal under the compassionate gaze of Christ.

Their dialogue, intense and impassioned, cuts through the silence. They speak of the daunting challenges that lie ahead – the convoluted pathways of forced labor that entangle innocent lives in a web of exploitation, the sinister networks of human trafficking that trade souls as commodities, and the insidious trap of debt bondage that shackles the vulnerable in a cycle of endless servitude. Their voices, laced with determination, echo the enduring spirit of William Wilberforce and Harriet Tubman, whose tireless efforts in the 18th and 19th centuries set the foundation for this ongoing battle.

As the night deepens, the group's focus sharpens. They recognize that this fight is not only against the overt acts of inhumanity but also against the systemic failings that allow such atrocities to thrive. The current immigration policies, they argue, often serve as unwitting accomplices to these crimes against humanity, leaving the most vulnerable exposed to the predations of modern-day slavers. The group acknowledges the need for a unified front, where churches, law enforcement, and community leaders collaborate to dismantle these criminal networks and reform the laws that inadvertently fuel this illicit trade.

Sarah, with a fire in her eyes, speaks of the need for an ethical response, a stance rooted in the Christian commitment to love and justice. It is a call to view each victim not as a statistic but as a reflection of God's image, deserving of rescue, restoration, and respect. She urges her fellow abolitionists to advocate for policies that uphold human rights and dignity, and to support organizations tirelessly working to bring light to the dark corners of exploitation.

As the assembly draws to a close, the group forms a circle, their hands clasped in a bond of solidarity. In this circle, they find strength, unity, and a shared vision for a world free from the chains of modern slavery. They leave with a renewed sense of purpose, ready to confront the darkness with the light of their faith, their actions fueled by the teachings of Christ to love and serve all.

This is not just a chapter in a book; it's a living testament to the enduring struggle for freedom and dignity. It's a narrative of hope, resilience, and the relentless pursuit of a world where every individual is valued, every voice is heard, and every life is free from the grasp of tyranny. This story, woven from the threads of past and present, is a clarion call to action – a reminder that the fight for freedom is far from over, and it's a battle that must be waged with the combined might of faith, love, and unwavering conviction.

"Unchained: How Christians Can Lead the Charge Against Slavery"

As Christians, this is especially true when it comes to the issue of slavery, which has been a scourge on humanity for centuries. Today, despite the progress that has been made in abolishing legal slavery, millions of people are still trapped in various forms of modern-day slavery. In modern times, forced labor, human trafficking, and debt bondage are forms of modern-day slavery that continue to plague societies around the world. These practices are often hidden in plain sight, and their victims are vulnerable people who are lured or forced into exploitation for the profit of others. In this report, we will examine what these practices are, how they are perpetrated, and how the efforts of abolitionists in the past are being undermined by current immigration policies. We will also discuss how Christian values need to be maintained in order to continue the fight against modern-day slavery. In the face of these challenges, it is essential to maintain Christian values in the fight against slavery. Christian teachings emphasize the importance of treating all people with love, compassion, and respect, regardless of their race, nationality, or social status. Christians believe that all people are created in the image of God and are therefore inherently valuable and deserving of dignity and respect. In the book of Galatians, chapter 3, verse 28, the apostle Paul writes, "There is neither Jew nor Gentile, neither slave nor free, nor is there male and female, for you are all one in Christ Jesus." This powerful statement has become a cornerstone of Christian theology, and speaks to the heart of the message of the Gospel: that all people are equal in the eyes of God, and that we are all called to love and serve one another. To fully appreciate the significance of Galatians 3:28, it is important to understand the historical and cultural context in which it was written. During the time of Paul, the world was deeply divided along lines of ethnicity, class, and gender. Jews and Gentiles were often at odds with one another, and slavery was an accepted and widely practiced institution in many societies. Women, too, were often treated as second-class citizens, with limited rights and opportunities. Moreover, the Bible is full of examples of God's concern for the oppressed and marginalized. Jesus himself demonstrated a particular concern for those who were most vulnerable, such as the poor, the sick, and the outcasts of society. As such, Christians have a unique role to play in the fight against modern-day slavery, using their faith as a motivation to work for justice and equality for all. Today, the message of Galatians 3:28 remains just as relevant and powerful as it was in the time of Paul. We live in a world that is still deeply divided along lines of ethnicity, culture, class, and gender. We see this in the ongoing struggles for racial justice, the persistence of gender inequality, and the continued oppression of marginalized communities around the world. Despite the efforts of slave abolitionists in England and America in the 19th century, slavery continues to exist in various forms today. This report will explore what forced labor, human trafficking, and debt bondage are in the modern world, the ways in which the work of slave abolitionists is being undermined by current immigration policies, and why it is essential to maintain Christian values in the fight against slavery.

THE ABOLITIONIST'S HANDBOOK: STRATEGIES AND SOLUTIONS FOR ENDING SLAVERY

During the 18th and 19th centuries, abolitionists in England and America dedicated themselves to eradicating the transatlantic slave trade and abolishing slavery. Their motivation stemmed from their Christian beliefs, which emphasized the equality of all individuals in the eyes of God. They felt compelled to fight for the freedom and dignity of every human being. To better understand the era that paved the way for these influential abolitionists, let's delve into their stories and explore the impact they had on society.

William Wilberforce, a British politician and devout Christian, was one of the leading abolitionists of his time. Wilberforce's personal reflections on God's word and his responsibilities in life produced not just an outward change in his conduct, but a profound change in his character and outlook.

In 1789, Wilberforce spoke his first anti-slavery speech before Parliament on May 12, 1789. He said, "So enormous, so dreadful, so irredeemable did (slavery's) wickedness appear that... I from this time determined that I would never rest till I affected its abolition!"

He dedicated over 20 years of his life in Parliament, tirelessly working towards the abolition of the slave trade. Finally, in 1807, his efforts bore fruit with the enactment of the Abolition of the Slave Trade Act. This significant legislation made it unlawful to engage in the buying and selling of slaves within the British Empire. However, it is important to note that the complete eradication of slavery took several more decades. It was not until 1833, just days before Wilberforce's passing, that the House of Commons passed the Slavery Abolition Act, which officially outlawed slavery throughout the British Empire.

In America, the abolitionist movement was led by figures such as Frederick Douglass, Harriet Tubman, and William Lloyd.

"'William Wilberforce, Frederick Douglass, Harriet Tubman, and William Lloyd'" were pioneers of the abolitionist movement who faced extreme resistance from the prevailing capitalistic mindset of the era. They dedicated their lives to fighting against slavery, advocating for the freedom of every individual to live without oppression. Their relentless efforts ultimately led to the abolition of slavery in the United Kingdom and the United States. However, the battle against slavery is ongoing. Even today, we witness modern forms of slavery, such as forced labor, human trafficking, and debt bondage, persisting in various parts of the world. Regrettably, these insidious forms of slavery often remain hidden and challenging to combat, further exacerbated by current immigration policies that undermine the work of these remarkable abolitionists.

'''Examples and Quotes from Wilberforce's Campaign'''

In the Parliament, Wilberforce faced strong opposition to his efforts to abolish the slave trade. Many argued that it was essential for the economy and that it was a necessary evil.

The concept of a necessary evil in the context of continued slave labor suggests that some people believed that the institution of slavery was necessary for the functioning of the economy at that time. They argued that the economic prosperity of certain industries, such as agriculture and manufacturing, heavily relied on the labor provided by enslaved individuals. They viewed slavery as an unfortunate but unavoidable means to maintain economic stability and growth.

However, it is important to note that this argument was strongly contested by abolitionists and other individuals who believed in the inherent rights and dignity of all human beings. They argued against the notion of slavery as a necessary evil, emphasizing the moral and ethical implications of treating fellow human beings as property. They advocated for the abolition of slavery based on principles of justice, equality, and human rights.

It is crucial to recognize that the concept of a necessary evil was a flawed justification used to perpetuate a system of oppression and exploitation. The arguments against it highlighted the importance of recognizing the fundamental rights and dignity of every individual, regardless of their race or social status.

Wilberforce took various measures to overcome the prevalent mindset of that era. He tirelessly advocated for the abolition of the slave trade, delivering powerful speeches and presenting evidence of the inhumane conditions faced by enslaved individuals.

To further illustrate his efforts, here are some facts and examples of the measures used by Wilberforce to battle slavery:

1. Formation of the Society for the Abolition of the Slave Trade: In 1787, Wilberforce co-founded the Society for the Abolition of the Slave Trade, a group dedicated to ending the transatlantic slave trade. The society worked to raise awareness, gather support, and lobby for legislative changes.

2. Parliamentary Campaigns: Wilberforce used his position as a Member of Parliament to introduce bills and motions

aimed at abolishing the slave trade. He presented evidence of the brutal treatment of enslaved individuals, highlighting the moral and humanitarian reasons for ending the practice.

3. Public Speaking: Wilberforce was known for his powerful oratory skills. He delivered numerous speeches in Parliament, captivating audiences with his passionate arguments against slavery. His speeches helped sway public opinion and gain support for the abolitionist cause.

4. Publication of "A Letter on the Abolition of the Slave Trade": In 1807, Wilberforce published a pamphlet titled "A Letter on the Abolition of the Slave Trade." This influential work outlined the moral and economic reasons for ending the slave trade and reached a wide audience, fur-

ther galvanizing support for the cause.

5. Collaboration with Other Abolitionists: Wilberforce worked closely with other prominent abolitionists, such as Thomas Clarkson and Granville Sharp. They formed alliances, shared information, and coordinated their efforts to maximize their impact in the fight against slavery.

These measures, along with Wilberforce's unwavering dedication and persuasive advocacy, played a crucial role in eventually leading to the abolition of the slave trade in the British Empire in 1807 and the emancipation of enslaved individuals in 1833.

"Wilberforce's campaign was driven by a deep sense of justice and compassion. He believed that every human being, regardless of their race or social status, deserved freedom and dignity."

"In the modern era, we have seen how the pursuit of profit and exploitation continues to plague impoverished and illiterate populations. Capitalistic and illegal desires have led to the exploitation of the world's poorest people, perpetuating a cycle of poverty and suffering."

"Wilberforce's legacy serves as a reminder that the fight against injustice and exploitation is ongoing. It is crucial for us to learn from history and work towards creating a more equitable and compassionate world for all."

Frederick Douglass was a former slave who escaped to freedom and became a leading abolitionist in the United States. He used his personal experience as a slave to speak out against the horrors of slavery and to advocate for its abolition. He was a powerful orator and writer, and his work helped to bring about the end of slavery in the United States.

Harriet Tubman was another former slave who escaped to freedom and then returned to the

South to help others escape. She made numerous trips to the South, leading slaves to freedom on the Underground Railroad. Tubman's bravery and determination made her a hero to many, and she continued to fight for the rights of African Americans even after the end of slavery.

William Lloyd Garrison was an American abolitionist who founded the American Anti-Slavery Society. He was a vocal advocate for the immediate abolition of slavery and worked tirelessly to spread the message of abolitionism throughout the United States. Garrison's work helped to create a groundswell of support for the abolitionist movement and paved the way for the eventual end of slavery in the United States.

Despite the work of these great abolitionists, modern forms of servitude still exist in many parts of the world. These forms of servitude or slavery often go unnoticed and are difficult to combat, as they are often hidden from view.

To make matters worse, current immigration policies are undermining the work of these great abolitionists.

Despite the tireless efforts of slave abolitionists in the 19th century, slavery continues to exist in various forms today. In fact, some of the current immigration policies of certain countries are undermining the work of slave abolitionists and perpetuating modern-day slavery.

For example, the United States' current immigration policies make it difficult for migrants and refugees to enter the country legally. As a result, many are forced to resort to illegal means to cross the border, making them vulnerable to human trafficking and forced labor. Moreover, the recent trend of separating families at the border has caused significant trauma and distress for both children and parents, putting them at increased risk of exploitation.

Similarly, the UK's recent changes to immigration laws have made it more challenging for victims of human trafficking to access support and services. As a result, many victims are left without the assistance they need to escape their situation and rebuild their lives.

Summarized: Forced labor, human trafficking, and debt bondage are serious forms of modern-day slavery that affect millions of people around the world. Despite the efforts of slave abolitionists in England and America in the 19th century, slavery continues to exist in various forms today. The work of slave abolitionists is being undermined by current immigration policies, perpetuating modern-day slavery to exist, albeit using different terminology.

Biblical Teachings on Justice and Freedom

In the fight against the shadows of modern slavery, our greatest light comes from the Word of God. This chapter delves into the scriptural teachings that empower and compel Christians to champion justice and freedom. It is a journey through the Bible, exploring how its timeless wisdom guides us in confronting the complex challenges of today's forms of slavery.

Relevant Passages and Teachings from the Bible

The Bible is replete with verses that champion the cause of the oppressed and call for justice. We begin with the profound words of Proverbs 31:8-9, which urge us to "Speak up for those who cannot speak for themselves... defend the rights of the poor and needy." This verse encapsulates the Christian mandate to be a voice for the voiceless, a directive that rings true in the context of modern slavery.

Another cornerstone scripture is Micah 6:8, which simplifies the call of God to "act justly and to love mercy and to walk humbly with your God." This verse encapsulates the essence of Christian living – a life marked by justice, compassion, and humility.

The Old Testament is filled with examples of God's heart for justice. In Isaiah 1:17, the call to "seek justice, rebuke the oppressor; defend the fatherless, plead for the widow" is clear and powerful. These verses are not mere suggestions; they are commands that resonate with the Christian's duty to stand against the exploitation and abuse inherent in modern slavery.

Jesus Christ, in His earthly ministry, exemplified the heart of God for the marginalized. His interactions with the outcasts of society were radical and counter-cultural. In Luke 4:18-19, Jesus declares His mission: "to proclaim good news to the poor... to proclaim freedom for the prisoners and recovery of sight for the blind, to set the oppressed free." This proclamation is a clarion call for Christians to follow in His footsteps.

Jesus' encounter with the Samaritan woman at the well (John 4:1-26) is a testament to His disregard for societal norms that marginalized certain groups. He reached out to those deemed unworthy, offering them dignity and hope. His life was a demonstration of love in action, a model for

Christians to emulate in the fight against slavery, which thrives on dehumanizing its victims.

The New Testament continues this theme of justice and love. In Galatians 3:28, Paul writes, "There is neither Jew nor Gentile, neither slave nor free, nor is there male and female, for you are all one in Christ Jesus." This verse underscores the equality and unity that Christ brings, breaking down the barriers that enable slavery.

Furthermore, 1 John 4:20 challenges us: "If anyone says, 'I love God,' and hates his brother, he is a liar; for he who does not love his brother whom he has seen cannot love God whom he has not seen." This powerful statement calls Christians to a love that transcends words and manifests in tangible actions against injustices like slavery.

The application of these principles in our modern context is clear. We are called to actively oppose all forms of modern slavery, recognizing the inherent worth and dignity in every person. Christians are to be at the forefront, advocating for laws and policies that protect the vulnerable, supporting organizations that fight against slavery, and raising awareness in our communities.

The legacy of abolitionists like Wilberforce and Tubman set a precedent for Christian activism. Today, the fight takes on new forms – forced labor, human trafficking, and debt bondage. These are the chains we must break, in the name of Christ.

Christians are uniquely positioned to address these issues. Churches can become centers of awareness and action, equipping members to recognize and report signs of modern slavery. Christian lawyers and activists can work to strengthen laws and support victims. Believers in every field can contribute – be it through prayer, advocacy, or direct action.

As we recognize the scale of modern slavery, the call for a unified Christian response is urgent. Churches, law enforcement, and legal professionals must collaborate to create a powerful front against these crimes against humanity. The synergy of spiritual fervor and practical action can create a formidable force against the darkness of slavery.

In conclusion, the Biblical teachings on justice and freedom are not just historical artifacts; they are living, breathing directives for today's battle against modern slavery. As Christians, we are called to carry the torch of justice, enlightened by the teachings of Scripture and empowered by the Spirit of God.

We end this chapter not with a period but with a call to action – a call to bring the love, justice, and freedom proclaimed in the Bible into the dark corners of our world, to shine a light on modern slavery, and to break the chains, in Jesus' name.

Interfaith Human Trafficking Toolkit

In the world's vast and often shadowed landscape, where the echoes of past struggles mingle with the cries of present injustices, a narrative unfolds—a tale of resilience, faith, and a relentless pursuit of freedom. This story begins with a guide, the 2019 Interfaith Human Trafficking Toolkit, a beacon of hope compiled by The Washington Inter-Religious Staff Community's Working Group on Human Trafficking. It is in these pages that our journey through history and faith begins, in the philosophical under-pinnings of Christian teachings and the relentless fight against modern-day slavery.

Once, in a time not so different from our own, great figures like William Wilberforce led a crusade against the abomination of slavery. His legacy, etched in the annals of history, serves as a torch in today's fight against forms of modern slavery—forced labor, human trafficking, and debt bondage. Hidden in plain sight, these practices ensnare the vulnerable, echoing the past's transgressions in today's global tapestry.

In the heart of this struggle, Christian values emerge as a clarion call to action. The Apostle Paul's words in Galatians 3:28, "There is neither Jew nor Gentile, neither slave nor free, nor is there male and female, for you are all one in Christ Jesus," resonate powerfully. This scripture, a cornerstone of Christian theology, speaks to the equality and inherent worth of all individuals, irrespective of their background or circumstances.

This message is further amplified in "Breaking Chains," a guide that delves into the biblical teachings on human dignity and the abolition of modern slavery. It implores, "In a world where injustice prevails, it is our Christian duty to be the bearers of hope and catalysts for freedom." This call to action is not just a historical echo but a contemporary imperative.

As the narrative unfolds, we encounter a group of Christians, leaders, activists, and concerned individuals, gathered around the Toolkit. They are the modern-day bearers of Wilberforce's torch, seeking to apply their faith to combat the darkness of slavery. Their dialogue is charged with moralistic reasoning, exploring the deep metaphysical implications of their mission.

The Toolkit becomes their roadmap, providing not only an understanding of human trafficking but also practical tools for action. They discuss the Toolkit's emphasis on strong migration governance and awareness of trafficking signs. It is a resource that transcends faith boundaries, yet is deeply rooted in Christian principles.

The group's discussion turns to the plight of immigrants and refugees, often the most susceptible to trafficking. They recall the story of Kyi and his family, who fled persecution only to find themselves ensnared in modern slavery. This story is a poignant reminder of the ongoing battle against exploitation and the need for compassionate intervention.

As the chapter progresses, the group grapples with the complexities of modern slavery. They recognize that, like in Wilberforce's time, this fight is not just against physical chains but against the metaphysical bonds of prejudice and ignorance. Their mission is deeply spiritual, guided by the teachings of Jesus Christ, who exemplified concern for the oppressed and marginalized.

The group embarks on various initiatives, mirroring the efforts of past abolitionists. They organize educational seminars, distribute resources, and engage in advocacy, all fueled by their faith and the teachings of the Bible. They are motivated by scriptures like 1 John 4:20, which emphasizes love and action.

As the saga nears its conclusion, the narrative takes on a reflective tone. The group recognizes that their fight against modern slavery is more than a physical struggle; it is a metaphysical journey towards a world where love, acceptance, and justice prevail. They understand that their actions, rooted in faith and guided by the legacy of abolitionists like Wilberforce, are part of a larger, divine narrative of justice and liberation.

The saga ends with a collective realization of their role as agents of change. They renew their commitment to fighting modern-day slavery, fortified by the lessons of the past and driven by a profound belief in the power of faith and action.

They stand united, a testament to the enduring spirit of humanity and the transformative power of faith in the relentless pursuit of freedom. As the saga of faith and freedom continues, our group of Christian activists, armed with the Interfaith Human Trafficking Toolkit, delves deeper into the heart of the modern abolitionist movement. The narrative, rich with metaphysical insights, explores the transformative power of uniting faith with action in the contemporary world. Uniting Faith and Action

In the dimly lit room, the group gathers around the Toolkit, each member reflecting on their unique journey to this moment. Their conversations reveal a tapestry of diverse backgrounds, yet all are united by a common mission: to eradicate the insidious plague of modern slavery.

Amidst the discussions, a new figure emerges, Sarah, a theologian who brings a deeper understanding of Christian teachings to the group. She speaks eloquently about the moral imperatives echoed in the Bible, drawing parallels between the struggles of past abolitionists and their current fight. "As Christians," she says, "our faith compels us not just to pray, but to act. We are God's instruments in bringing about justice and freedom."

The group nods in agreement, inspired by Sarah's words. They delve into a discussion about the application of Christian values in practical terms. The Toolkit serves as a guide, but it is their faith that fuels their determination. They plan outreach programs, educational workshops, and advocacy campaigns, each initiative infused with a sense of moral urgency and guided by their Christian ethos.

As the narrative progresses, the group's efforts begin to bear fruit. They successfully organize a series of community events, bringing awareness to the issue of human trafficking. Their approach is unique, blending historical abolitionist strategies with modern methods. They create a bridge between the past and present, showing how the principles of equality and justice remain constant through the ages.

In one powerful scene, the group hosts a candlelight vigil to honor the victims of modern slavery. The flickering candles cast a warm glow, symbolizing hope in the darkness. Here, they recite passages from both the Bible and speeches by historical figures like Wilberforce, creating a profound connection between their faith and their fight against slavery.

The group's journey is not without challenges. They face skepticism and apathy from some community members, mirroring the obstacles faced by past abolitionists. Yet, their resolve only strengthens. Guided by their faith, they navigate these challenges, using their moral compass to stay true to their mission.

Sarah's theological insights continue to inspire the group. She speaks about the Christian duty to love and serve the least among us, drawing from scriptures such as Matthew 25:40, "Truly I tell you, whatever you did for one of the least of these brothers and sisters of mine, you did for me." This scripture becomes a rallying cry for the group, a reminder of their higher purpose.

As the saga nears its conclusion, the narrative reflects on the journey undertaken by the group. From the historical echoes of abolitionism to the pressing realities of modern slavery, their crusade has been a testament to the enduring power of faith in action.

In the final scene, the group stands together, looking out over a sea of faces at a community event. They have ignited a spark of awareness and compassion in their community. Their efforts, rooted in Christian values and the legacy of past abolitionists, have created ripples of change, echoing the call for freedom and justice across time and space.

The story closes with a sense of hope and a call to action. The fight against modern slavery continues, but the group's journey has shown that when faith and action converge, the chains of oppression can be broken. The narrative is more than a story; it's a living testament to the power of faith in the relentless pursuit of freedom.

The Interfaith Crusade Against Modern Slavery

The Interfaith Toolkit to End Trafficking, compiled by The Washington Inter-Religious Staff Community's Working Group on Human Trafficking, serves as a foundational guide. It empowers faith leaders, organizations, and houses of worship in the fight against human trafficking, uniting Islamic, Christian, Buddhist, Hindu, Jewish, and Unitarian Universalist leaders around the shared principles of human dignity, ending injustice, and caring for the marginalized.

In the labyrinth of a world fragmented by differing beliefs, there unfolds a gripping saga of unity against the sinister tide of modern slavery. Here, faith communities converge, not in mere dialogue, but in a dynamic alliance, to battle this age-old scourge with newfound fervor.

In the bustling streets of New York, leaders from various faiths convene clandestinely, their meeting marked by an urgent mission—to forge a bond strong enough to challenge the insidious networks of modern slavery. They recognize that their paths to the divine might differ, but their destination is unified—a world free from chains and shackles.

A mosaic of community outreach programs and advocacy campaigns emerges, serving as beacons of hope. In a small village in India, a church and a temple collaborate to liberate bonded laborers, demonstrating the power of unity in diversity.

This narrative concludes with a strong affirmation of the power and potential of interfaith collaboration in the fight against modern slavery. By uniting under the shared banners of justice, compassion, and human dignity, diverse faith communities can significantly contribute to the abolition of slavery. This chapter calls for a continued commitment to interfaith dialogue, collaboration, and action, recognizing that in our unity lies our strength.

The Crusade of Unity: An Interfaith Saga Against Human Trafficking

In the shadowed corners of our world, where the sinister trade of human lives thrives, a remarkable saga unfolds—a tale of unity, courage, and hope. It's a story that transcends boundaries, beliefs, and backgrounds, bringing together an unlikely alliance of faiths in a resolute fight against modern slavery.

In the heart of Santa Barbara County, under the auspices of the District Attorney's Office, a unique collaborative emerges. It's a mosaic of faith community members, law enforcement agencies, non-profits, and faith-based organizations, all united in a singular mission—to dismantle the dark web of human trafficking. This Interfaith

Collaborative Against Human Trafficking isn't just a coalition; it's a beacon of hope. Through education and empowerment, this group galvanizes local action against the scourge of sex and labor trafficking, adopting a victim-centered approach that resonates with compassion and understanding.

But the saga doesn't end there. Across the globe, UNICEF, a vanguard in child protection, crafts an extraordinary tool—the Interfaith Toolkit to End Trafficking. This toolkit isn't just a collection of strategies; it's a manifesto of unity. It brings together Islamic, Christian, Buddhist, Hindu, Jewish, and Unitarian Universalist leaders, all rallying around the noble cause of human dignity and the end of injustice. This is a call to arms, echoing through temples, churches, mosques, and synagogues, urging a united stand against the trafficking and exploitation of innocent children.

Meanwhile, the Faith Alliance Against Slavery and Trafficking (FAAST) weaves its narrative—a strategic alliance of Christian organizations working in unison to obliterate the chains of slavery. FAAST is more than an organization; it's a movement. With a mission to mobilize and equip communities globally, it represents a tapestry of Christian churches, denominations, and academic institutions, all marching to the drumbeat of freedom and restoration. This alliance is a testament to the power of faith-driven collaboration, proving that when beliefs align for a cause greater than themselves, the impact can be monumental.

These stories, these chapters of interfaith unity, are imbued with a spirit that defies the darkness. They demonstrate the profound impact of collaboration across faith lines. In these efforts, there's a shared recognition—a truth that transcends religious doctrines—that every human being has an inherent worth that must be protected, respected, and cherished.

As this saga of interfaith collaboration against human trafficking unfolds, it brings to light an undeniable truth: in the fight against the evils of slavery, our diversity is our strength. The unity of faiths creates a formidable force, a chorus of diverse voices singing the same hymn of freedom, justice, and hope. This is a story of resilience, a narrative where empathy and action interlace, a testament to the enduring spirit of humanity that refuses to turn a blind eye to suffering and injustice.

In conclusion, this is not merely a recounting of events; it is an invitation—a call to all faiths and people to join this crusade of unity. It is a reminder that in the darkest of times, the most brilliant of lights can emerge from the coming together of different faiths, united in their resolve to end the tragedy of human trafficking.

The Faith Alliance Against Slavery and Trafficking (FAAST) is a strategic alliance of Christian organizations working globally to combat slavery and restore survivors. Their mission is to mobilize and equip communities, fostering collaboration between Christian churches, denominations, universities, and communities to confront human trafficking.

Despite the kaleidoscope of beliefs, these warriors of faith find common ground in their ethical and moral values. They are driven by a shared vision to uphold human dignity, justice, and freedom. Their unity becomes their most potent weapon, transforming diverse perspectives into a source of strength.

As they strategize, their plans are ambitious. They envision a world where advocacy is not just a whisper but a resounding cry for justice. By pooling resources, they launch far-reaching campaigns, amplifying their message with the collective power of their faiths.

In the darkest corners of exploitation, these interfaith champions bring light. They establish holistic support programs where victims of modern slavery find refuge and a path to healing. In these sanctuaries, survivors find solace in a Rabbi's prayer, strength in a Priest's words, and hope in an Imam's blessing.

As the chapter nears its end, it becomes clear that this saga is far from over. The interfaith alliance stands resolute, their unity not just their strength but their most formidable weapon. They pledge to continue their crusade, their conviction unwavering, their spirits undeterred.

The chapter concludes with a clarion call to faith communities worldwide. It's a summons to join this grand alliance, to contribute to this noble cause. It's a recognition that in the fight against modern slavery, every voice matters, every hand counts. This isn't just a chapter in a book; it's a chapter in history, a narrative of hope, resilience, and the relentless pursuit of freedom.

"The New Underground Railroad: Rescuing Victims of Human Trafficking

In the shadowed corridors of the modern world, a battle endures, often unseen yet pervasive in its grip on humanity. This saga, woven from the fabric of both history and the present, tells a tale of a fight against an age-old evil that refuses to perish—modern slavery. In its many forms, like forced labor, human trafficking, and debt bondage, it mocks our moral progress, questioning the very essence of our humanity. This story, though set in our times, is deeply anchored in the heroic deeds of past abolitionists like William Wilberforce and Harriet Tubman, whose unwavering dedication to freedom lights our path today.

As the narrative unfolds, we witness a world paradoxically advanced yet still chained to primitive injustices. In bustling metropolises and remote villages alike, the specter of slavery looms, cloaked in the guise of normalcy. Here, individuals are not bound by iron chains, but by the invisible shackles of coercion, deceit, and exploitation. It's a world where the desperate cries for help often go unheard, buried under the din of global indifference.

In this modern crusade against slavery, a new breed of abolitionists emerges, fueled by a timeless doctrine of love and justice, as taught by Christ.

They draw inspiration from the teachings of 1 John 4:20 and Galatians 3:28, scriptures that resonate with the call for universal brotherhood and equality under the divine gaze of God. These modern-day warriors, diverse in their faiths and backgrounds, unite under a shared conviction – to end the tyranny of slavery in all its forms.

Amid this backdrop, our tale centers on Sarah, a fervent advocate whose soul burns with a passion for justice. Guided by her Christian faith, she sees beyond race and gender, recognizing the divine spark in every individual. Sarah, along with her fellow abolitionists, confronts the daunting task of battling the insidious networks of modern slavery, a fight that is as much about liberating the physical body as it is about freeing the bound spirit.

Their journey is fraught with challenges, each step forward met with the resistance of deeply entrenched interests and the apathy of a world slow to change. They navigate through the complexities of forced labor, where men, women, and children are reduced to mere tools of profit. They delve into the dark realms of human trafficking, where lives are traded with chilling nonchalance. They expose the cruel reality of debt bondage, where freedom becomes an elusive dream, forever out of reach.

Yet, amidst this bleak landscape, there is hope. The resolute spirit of the abolitionists, armed with the transformative power of faith and love, begins to kindle a flame of change. They rally communities, educate the uninformed, and empower the vulnerable. They lobby for policy changes, provide safe havens for the rescued, and tirelessly advocate for the silenced and forgotten.

As the narrative reaches its crescendo, we see a world slowly awakening to the plight of the enslaved. Sarah and her comrades, through their unyielding efforts, begin to dismantle the barriers of ignorance and apathy. They build bridges of empathy and understanding, creating a collective consciousness that recognizes the inherent worth and dignity of every human being.

The saga concludes not with an end, but with a call to action—a clarion call that resonates across faiths and nations. It beckons each of us to join this noble crusade, to contribute in our own way to this fight for freedom and dignity. For in this battle against modern slavery, every effort counts, every voice matters. It's a journey not just towards the liberation of the enslaved but also towards the redemption of our own humanity.

In a world where the echoes of history still resonate, where the battles for freedom are fought on the battlegrounds of faith, love, and courage, this is a story that intertwines the past and the present. Inspired by the unwavering spirit of giants like Wilberforce and Tubman, it serves as a powerful reminder that the fight for liberation is far from over. With resilience as their armor and hope as their guiding light, our protagonists embark on a journey that unveils the true meaning of freedom—a world where every soul is cherished, honored, and unshackled.

Slavery in the 18 and 19th centuries is different than what is becoming a major international human rights form of injustice that violates each victims god given value as human beings. With the work of the slavery abolitionist making the sell of another human a crime, it leaves only criminals to be the perpetrateping countries is what Christians should find as a priority and bring the force of a unified front by churches,Law enforcement and prosecution leaders. Forced labor, human trafficking, and debt bondage are all forms of modern day slavery that continue to exist in various parts of the world. Forced labor involves individuals being coerced or forced to work against their will, often under the threat of violence or punishment.

Human trafficking is a grave crime that involves various methods to exploit individuals. It encompasses the recruitment, transportation, transfer, or harboring of people through the use of force, threats, coercion, abduction, fraud, deception, abuse of power, or taking advantage of their vulnerability.

One form of human trafficking is debt bondage, where individuals are trapped in a cycle of servitude due to an insurmountable debt. In this scenario, victims are coerced into working to repay a debt that often accumulates interest and becomes impossible to fully repay. This exploitative practice perpetuates a cycle of debt and servitude, leaving victims trapped in a state of forced labor.

For instance, imagine a scenario where a person from a disadvantaged background is promised a job opportunity abroad. However, upon arrival, they are informed that they owe a substantial amount of money for transportation, accommodation, and other expenses. The traffickers then force them into labor, manipulating their vulnerability and using the debt as a means of control.

It is crucial to understand the various tactics employed in human trafficking, such as debt bondage, to raise awareness and combat this heinous crime. By shedding light on these examples and providing additional information, we can reinforce the narrative and emphasize the urgency of addressing this global issue.

Despite the efforts of slave abolitionists in England and America, these forms of modern day slavery persist, often in the shadows and hidden from public view. The fight against modern day slavery is further undermined by current immigration policies, which often fail to adequately protect vulnerable individuals and may even exacerbate their vulnerability to exploitation. As Christians, we must maintain our commitment to the values of justice, compassion, and love for all people. We must speak out against the injustices of modern day slavery and work towards its eradication. This includes advocating for policies that protect the rights and dignity of all individuals, as well as supporting organizations that work towards the prevention, rescue, and rehabilitation of victims of modern day slavery. Furthermore, we must also examine our own actions and behaviors, ensuring that we are not complicit in perpetuating systems of exploitation and oppression. We must strive to live out the values of Christ, seeking to love and serve all people regardless of their race, nationality, or social status. Christians are to be opposed to forced labor, human trafficking, and debt bondage as modern day forms of slavery that continue to exist in various parts of the world. As Christians, we must maintain our commitment to the values of justice, compassion, and love for all people and work towards the eradication of modern day slavery in all its forms.

COMBATING MODERN SLAVERY

"Combating Modern Slavery: The Urgent Need for a Renewed Abolitionist Movement," addresses the critical issue of modern slavery, particularly focusing on forced labor. This form of modern-day slavery, characterized by coercion, deception, and exploitation, mirrors the historical atrocities that abolitionists like William Wilberforce fought against.

Modern slavery, specifically forced labor, represents a profound violation of human rights, necessitating a revitalized abolitionist movement that integrates faith-based perspectives, with modern strategies to effectively combat this global scourge.

Historical Context and Legacy of Abolitionism:

Quote: "You may choose to look the other way but you can never say again that you did not know." - William Wilberforce.

Modern-day slavery and forced labor are grave human rights violations that plague our society. This thesis delves into the dynamics of forced labor, exploring its definition, manifestations, and the urgent need for abolitionist efforts. Drawing from contemporary authors and experts in the field, it highlights the mechanisms of exploitation and emphasizes the call for immediate action to combat this global epidemic.

Forced labor, also known as labor trafficking, is a pernicious form of modern slavery that involves individuals being coerced into work through deceit, intimidation, or violence. This thesis examines the various industries affected by forced labor, such as agriculture, manufacturing, and domestic work. It underscores the inhumane working conditions and the cycle of abuse and exploitation that victims endure. The insights from contemporary authors shed light on the urgent need for abolitionist action to dismantle these trafficking networks.

The perpetuation of forced labor is deeply rooted in systemic issues such as poverty, lack of education, and inadequate legal protections. This thesis highlights the complex nature of labor trafficking, as discussed by experts in the field. It emphasizes the importance of policy reform, international cooperation, and grassroots mobilization in the fight against forced labor. The insights from contemporary authors provide valuable perspectives on the multifaceted approach required to combat this global crisis.

The fight against forced labor necessitates a comprehensive approach that includes legal action, international cooperation, and grassroots mobilization. This thesis draws on the insights of contemporary authors to underscore the urgency of addressing the root causes and manifestations of labor trafficking. It emphasizes the moral imperative of collective efforts to end this form of modern slavery, as highlighted by these leading voices in the fight against human trafficking.

Human trafficking, encompassing forced labor, sexual exploitation, and organ trafficking, is a severe violation of human dignity and rights. This thesis explores the intricacies of human trafficking, reflecting on the perspectives and insights from modern authors who emphasize the need for abolitionist efforts in our society. It underscores the urgent need for comprehensive and collaborative strategies to combat this global crisis.

Debt bondage, a sinister form of modern slavery, traps individuals in a vicious cycle of debt and forced labor. This thesis explores the phenomenon of debt bondage, incorporating examples and quotes from contemporary authors who address the need for abolitionist efforts to eradicate this scourge.

Debt bondage, a modern form of slavery, forces individuals to work off debts under exploitative conditions. This thesis examines the nature of debt bondage, its prevalence in various industries, and the voices of modern authors advocating for its abolition. It highlights the manipulation of debts and exorbitant interest rates that perpetuate this form of exploitation.

Debt bondage is not restricted to any single industry but is prevalent in agriculture, manufacturing, mining, and other sectors. This thesis draws on the insights of contemporary authors to shed light on the cycle of debt bondage and the challenges faced by victims. It emphasizes the need for stronger laws, better enforcement, and increased awareness to combat this form of modern slavery.

Addressing debt bondage requires a multi-faceted approach involving legal, economic, and social interventions. The insights from modern authors underline the importance of stronger laws, better enforcement, and increased awareness to prevent and combat debt bondage. They emphasize the need to empower victims and provide viable alternatives to escape this cycle of exploitation. The voices of these authors serve as a clarion call for action against this form of modern slavery, urging us to restore dignity and freedom to its victims.

Understanding the Modern Slavery Crisis

As we further explore the depths of modern slavery, it becomes clear that this crisis is not just a remnant of the past but a present and growing evil. It demands a response that is informed, compassionate, and relentless.

Awareness is the first step in the battle against modern slavery. By understanding the magnitude and complexity of this issue, we can begin to dismantle the systems that allow it to thrive. This includes education on the signs of human trafficking, understanding how to report suspicions, and knowing how to support survivors.

The globalization of economies has inadvertently facilitated the spread of modern slavery. Supply chains often span multiple countries, making it difficult to track the use of forced labor. As consumers and Christians, we are called to advocate for transparency and ethical practices in business and trade. Our purchasing power can be a tool for change, demanding products and services free from the taint of exploitation.

The fight against modern slavery cannot be waged by individuals alone; it requires collective action. Churches, faith-based organizations, NGOs, and governments must work together to create a formidable front against traffickers and slaveholders. This collaboration is essential for effective intervention, rescue operations, and policy advocacy.

Policy change is crucial in combating modern slavery. Laws that strengthen border controls, protect victims' rights, and penalize traffickers are necessary to curb this crisis. Advocacy for these policies is an essential role that Christians can play, bringing moral and ethical considerations to the forefront of political discourse.

As followers of Christ, our response to modern slavery must be rooted in compassion and justice. The parable of the Good Samaritan (Luke 10:25-37) is a poignant reminder of our duty to help those who are suffering, regardless of their background or circumstances. This parable calls us to action, to be neighbors to those who are most vulnerable to exploitation and abuse.

The journey does not end with rescue. Survivors of modern slavery need support to heal and rebuild their lives. This includes access to medical care, psychological counseling, legal assistance, and vocational training. Churches and faith communities can play a vital role in this recovery process, offering a supportive environment where survivors can find refuge, hope, and a new beginning.

In conclusion, understanding the modern slavery crisis is a complex but necessary step in eradicating this evil. As Christians, we are called not only to empathize with the suffering but to actively participate in the liberation of the oppressed. This chapter is a call to arms, urging us to use our resources, influence, and faith to fight against the forces of exploitation and human trafficking.

Let us move forward with the knowledge that our actions, grounded in love and justice, can make a difference in this fight. We are called to be the light in the darkness, to seek out the lost and the broken, and to bring them into the safety and love of God's embrace. May our efforts contribute to a world where freedom is not a privilege but a right afforded to every human being

Rescuing Victims of Human Trafficking

The New Underground Railroad: Rescuing Victims of Human Trafficking

Human trafficking is one of the fastest growing criminal industries in the world. It is a modern day form of slavery that involves the exploitation of vulnerable individuals for forced labor, sexual exploitation, or other forms of exploitation. According to the International Labor Organization, there are an estimated 25 million victims of human trafficking worldwide. In this report, we will explore the issue of human trafficking from a Christian perspective and discuss the concept of the new underground railroad a movement of individuals and organizations working to rescue victims of human trafficking and provide them with the support they need to heal and rebuild their lives. As Christians, we are called to love our neighbors as ourselves and to care for the most vulnerable members of our society. Human trafficking is a violation of human dignity and a direct affront to God's command to love one another. It is a form of evil that must be opposed by all people of good will, and especially by Christians who seek to follow in the footsteps of Jesus Christ. The concept of the new underground railroad draws inspiration from the historical underground railroad, which was a network of secret routes and safe houses used by African American slaves to escape to freedom in the 19th century. The new underground railroad seeks to provide a similar pathway to freedom for victims of human trafficking. It involves a network of individuals and organizations who work together to identify victims of trafficking, provide them with safe places to stay, and connect them with the resources they need to recover and rebuild their lives. The new underground railroad operates on a few key principles, which are rooted in Christian values. First and foremost, it is a movement based on compassion and love for one's neighbor. Those involved in the movement are driven by a desire to help those who are suffering and to offer them hope for a better future. They understand that the work they do is not only necessary but also a reflection of their faith in God.

Advocacy Strategies for Christians

In this pivotal chapter, we turn our focus to the power of advocacy as a tool for Christians to combat modern slavery. The chapter aims to equip believers with strategies to influence policy, build coalitions, and effectively engage with lawmakers, drawing upon the rich heritage of Christian activism and the contemporary challenges of the modern slavery crisis.

Understanding the Power of Advocacy

Advocacy is more than just voicing concerns; it's about creating systemic change. By amplifying the voices of survivors and advocating for their rights, Christians can make a tangible impact in the fight against modern slavery.

Effective Advocacy Techniques:

- **Storytelling:** Sharing survivors' stories can be a powerful tool for advocacy, creating empathy and driving action.

- **Building Relationships:** Establishing connections with stakeholders, including policymakers, NGOs, and survivor groups, is crucial for effective advocacy.

- **Utilizing Social Media:** In today's digital age, social media platforms are instrumental in raising awareness and mobilizing support for anti-slavery initiatives.

Successful advocacy campaigns, like those led by William Wilberforce against historical slavery, provide inspirational models. Their strategies, adapted to modern contexts, can guide today's Christians in advocating for systemic change.

Building Alliances and Coalitions

Collaboration amplifies impact. By forming alliances with organizations and individuals committed to ending modern slavery, Christians can leverage collective strength.

Strategies for Collaboration:

- **Identifying Partners:** Seek out like-minded groups, such as NGOs, community organizations, and other faith-based entities, that share a commitment to ending modern slavery.

- **Establishing Partnerships:** Foster mutual trust and establish clear objectives to ensure effective collaboration.

- **Fostering Cooperation:** Regular communication and joint initiatives can strengthen alliances, creating a unified front against slavery.

Engaging with Lawmakers and Influencing Legislation

To effect lasting change, Christians must engage with the legislative process. Influencing policy is a critical aspect of advocacy.

Strategies for Legislative Engagement:

- **Contacting Representatives:** Encourage Christians to reach out to their lawmakers to express concerns about modern slavery and support for anti-slavery legislation.

- **Attending Hearings and Advocacy Events:** Active participation in political processes raises the profile of anti-slavery efforts.

- **Grassroots Mobilization:** Organize community-driven campaigns to support anti-slavery bills, demonstrating broad public support for these issues.

The New Underground Railroad: A Christian Response to Human Trafficking

Echoing the commitment and values of the historical Underground Railroad, this modern equivalent embodies Christian principles of compassion, dignity, and justice. It is a movement that seeks to rescue and rehabilitate victims of human trafficking, reflecting Christ's teachings on loving and serving the most vulnerable in society.

In advocating for the eradication of modern slavery, Christians are guided by principles of justice, compassion, and love for all, as emphasized in 1 John 4:20 and Galatians 3:28. These values underpin our approach to addressing contemporary forms of slavery, including forced labor, human trafficking, and debt bondage.

This chapter is a call to action for Christians to rise as modern-day abolitionists. Through strategic advocacy, building alliances, and engaging with lawmakers, believers can be instrumental in the fight against modern slavery. As we seek to live out our faith, let us remember that advocacy is not just a response to injustice but a reflection of Christ's love and command to be agents of change in the world.

As we further explore the role of Christians in the advocacy against modern slavery, we dive into the practical aspects of this fight, understanding that our actions must be rooted in faith and driven by a commitment to justice and righteousness.

In this battle, our faith is not a passive stance but a dynamic force. We are reminded of 2 Corinthians 5:20, which calls us to be ambassadors for Christ. In this ambassadorial role, our advocacy is not just about changing policies but about transforming hearts and societies.

Today's slavery differs from historical slavery in its insidious and hidden nature. Christians must be informed about the complexities of issues like forced labor, sex trafficking, and debt bondage. Understanding these issues allows us to advocate more effectively and to speak with knowledge and compassion.

Awareness within our churches and communities is vital. By organizing talks, seminars, and discussion forums, we can educate fellow believers about the realities of modern slavery. This awareness is the first step in mobilizing the church community to take action.

The global Christian community is a powerful network that can be leveraged for advocacy. By uniting with other churches and Christian organizations, we can create a strong, collective voice that can influence policymakers and bring about change.

As Christians, our advocacy should extend to supporting policies that promote ethical practices in business and government. This includes pushing for laws that ensure transparency in supply chains and hold corporations accountable for any involvement in modern slavery.

True advocacy goes beyond policy change; it also involves supporting the victims and the vulnerable. This can be done through supporting shelters, rehabilitation programs, and providing legal assistance to survivors of modern slavery.

In all our efforts, prayer is a powerful tool. We must commit our advocacy work to God, seeking His guidance and wisdom. Prayer rallies and intercessory groups can be powerful in bringing about spiritual breakthroughs in the fight against slavery.

Our journey concludes with a reaffirmation of the Christian duty to act against modern slavery. As followers of Christ, we are called to love our neighbors, stand against injustice, and be the voice for the voiceless. Our advocacy, rooted in Christian values and driven by faith, can make a significant impact in the fight against modern slavery.

By engaging in advocacy, building strategic alliances, and influencing legislation, we can contribute to the dismantling of modern slavery systems. Let this chapter serve not just as a guide, but as a catalyst for action, inspiring Christians to step up as modern-day abolitionists, advocating for freedom, justice, and the restoration of dignity to all those ensnared by the chains of modern slavery.

Despite the efforts of slave abolitionists in England and America, these forms of modern-day slavery persist, often in the shadows and hidden from public view. The fight against modern-day slavery is further undermined by current immigration policies, which often fail to adequately protect vulnerable individuals and may even exacerbate their vulnerability to exploitation. As Christians, we must maintain our commitment to the values of justice, compassion, and love for all people. We must speak out against the injustices of modern-day slavery and work towards its eradication. This includes advocating for policies that protect the rights and dignity of all individuals, as well as supporting organizations that work towards the prevention, rescue, and rehabilitation of victims of modern-day slavery. Furthermore, we must also examine our own actions and behaviors, ensuring that we are not complicit in perpetuating systems of exploitation and oppression. We must strive to live out the values of Christ, seeking to love and serve all people regardless of their race, nationality, or social status. Christians are to be opposed to forced labor, human trafficking, and debt bondage as modern-day forms of slavery that continue to exist in various parts of the world. As Christians, we must maintain our commitment to the values of justice, compassion, and love for all people and work towards the eradication of modern-day slavery in all its forms.

Organ Trafficking: A Hidden Plague

In the shadowy corners of the world, a sinister trade thrives, veiled from public gaze yet pervasive in its reach. This is the world of organ trafficking, a realm where human beings are reduced to mere commodities, bought and sold for profit. This narrative delves into the labyrinthine darkness of organ trafficking, a lesser-discussed yet critical facet of human trafficking, often overshadowed by its more publicized counterparts: sex and labor trafficking.

The tale unfolds with a glimpse into the global illicit organ trade, a lucrative enterprise for transnational organized crime groups. Driven by high demand and marked by low law enforcement rates, organ traffickers profit in the shadows. Their destructive medical footprint, however, leaves indelible scars – vulnerable populations, termed "donors," and first-world beneficiaries, known as "recipients," are ensnared in a web of severe exploitation, facing a lifetime of health consequences.

This form of illicit trade also challenges the private sector, particularly the financial industry, which becomes an unknowing conduit for its facilitation. However, with appropriate training and heightened awareness, financial institutions may play a pivotal role in unmasking organ traders by tracing the financial trails they leave behind.

Diving deeper, we explore the perplexing dynamics of this crime. The World Health Organization (WHO) estimates that approximately 10,000 kidneys are traded on the black market annually, equating to more than one every hour. These staggering numbers, when juxtaposed against the average wait times for organs in developed countries, paint a stark picture of the demand diverted to black markets.

Trafficked organs, once procured, can be transplanted in the most reputable hospitals, yet often, clandestine makeshift operating rooms serve as the venues for these illicit transplants. Traffickers, preying on the vulnerability of both donors and recipients, create a complex equation of exploitation and desperation.

How does organ trafficking fit within the broader spectrum of human trafficking? The Palermo Protocol of 2000 incorporates organ trafficking within its definition, categorizing it alongside sexual exploitation, forced labor, and slavery. This inclusion broadens the lexicon of human trafficking and highlights the multifaceted nature of this global issue.

The legal landscape surrounding organ trafficking is fraught with complexities. While most countries outlaw the buying and selling of organs, few legislate against citizens traveling abroad to acquire organs. This gap in the law creates a fertile ground for "transplant tourism," a phenomenon catered to by companies operating under the guise of legality.

The financial magnitude of this illegal trade is staggering, with estimates suggesting that it generates between $840 million to $1.7 billion annually. However, detecting related financial activities poses significant challenges for law enforcement and anti-money laundering professionals. The transnational nature of the crime, coupled with the savvy of its perpetrators, who often utilize shell companies and sanitized public offerings, makes tracking these operations an arduous task.

This saga of organ trafficking is not just a tale of crime and exploitation; it's a call to action. It urges law enforcement, the financial sector, healthcare professionals, and the public to join forces in combating this insidious form of human trafficking. By raising awareness, strengthening laws, and enhancing international cooperation, we can begin to dismantle the networks that perpetuate this trade and protect those vulnerable to its predatory practices.

In the fight against organ trafficking, every step taken is a step closer to a world where human dignity prevails over profit, where life is valued more than lucre. This narrative, weaving through the dark alleys of organ trafficking, shines a light on a hidden crisis, beckoning us to stand united in this crucial battle for humanity.

As the narrative of organ trafficking unfolds, it becomes increasingly apparent that this clandestine trade is not merely a criminal issue but a profound moral crisis. The story takes us through the journey of those caught in the snare of this illicit market - the desperate 'donors,' often from impoverished backgrounds, and the 'recipients,' driven by dire medical needs but ensnared in an ethical quandary.

The saga delves into the lives of the donors, individuals often coerced into parting with their organs due to extreme financial need. Their stories are tales of exploitation and despair. Unaware of the health risks and long-term consequences, these donors are left with lasting physical and emotional scars. The narrative paints a vivid picture of their struggles, highlighting the need for a global awakening to this hidden human rights violation.

On the other end of this spectrum are the recipients. Driven by the urgency of their health conditions and the inadequacies of legal organ donation systems, they find themselves in a moral labyrinth. The narrative explores the complex emotions and ethical dilemmas faced by these individuals, often unaware of the full implications of their decisions on the lives of the donors.

Healthcare professionals find themselves at the crossroads of this crisis. Bound by the Hippocratic Oath yet confronted with the realities of this black-market trade, they face moral dilemmas. The story highlights the role of ethical healthcare practices and the need for stringent protocols to ensure that organ transplants are carried out legally and ethically.

The global response to organ trafficking is multifaceted. International organizations, governments, and non-profits are working tirelessly to combat this trade. The narrative details the efforts of entities like the United Nations and the World Health Organization in framing policies and protocols to curb organ trafficking. It underscores the importance of international treaties and the need for harmonized laws across nations to effectively combat this transnational crime.

A critical aspect of tackling organ trafficking is tracing and disrupting the financial flows that fuel this trade. The narrative explores the role of anti-money laundering professionals and financial institutions in identifying and reporting suspicious transactions related to organ trafficking. It illustrates the complexity of tracking these financial trails and the need for robust international cooperation in this endeavor.

Raising awareness is a vital tool in combating organ trafficking. The narrative spotlights the role of media, activists, and educators in bringing this issue to the forefront of public consciousness. It highlights successful campaigns and initiatives that have brought attention to this issue, mobilizing public opinion and spurring legislative action.

In conclusion, the saga of organ trafficking is a call for a unified global response. It requires cooperation across borders, sectors, and disciplines. From legal reforms and enhanced law enforcement to ethical medical practices and financial vigilance, every effort counts. The narrative concludes with a powerful call to action, urging readers to become part of the solution – to advocate, educate, and collaborate in the fight against this heinous form of human trafficking.

This comprehensive exploration into the world of organ trafficking not only sheds light on a hidden crisis but also inspires hope – hope for a future where such exploitation is a thing of the past, and human dignity and ethics triumph over greed and desperation.

Continuing the narrative, we shift our focus to the Christian perspective on the atrocity of organ harvesting. Within Christian teachings, the sanctity of human life and the dignity of the human body are central tenets. These beliefs, rooted in scripture, provide a moral compass that stands in stark opposition to the exploitation inherent in organ harvesting.

From a Christian standpoint, the human body is seen as a temple of the Holy Spirit, to be treated with respect and honor. 1 Corinthians 6:19-20 states, "Do you not know that your bodies are temples of the Holy Spirit, who is in you, whom you have received from God? You are not your own; you were bought at a price. Therefore honor God with your bodies." This passage underscores the belief that the human body is sacred and not to be exploited for commercial gain.

Similarly, the commandment "You shall not murder" (Exodus 20:13) underpins the Christian stance against taking life unjustly. The practice of organ harvesting, often associated with coercion, violence, and even murder, is fundamentally at odds with this commandment.

The parables of Jesus often speak to the value of each individual and the importance of protecting the vulnerable. The Parable of the Good Samaritan (Luke 10:25-37) is a powerful example. In this story, a Samaritan helps a man who has been beaten and left for dead, while others pass by without assisting. This parable teaches the importance of caring for those in need, regardless of their background. In the context of organ harvesting, this parable speaks to the responsibility of Christians to protect and aid those vulnerable to exploitation.

Another significant teaching is the concept of loving one's neighbor as oneself (Mark 12:31). This principle calls for empathy and action against injustices inflicted upon others, including the exploitation inherent in organ trafficking and harvesting.

Throughout history, Christians have been at the forefront of humanitarian and social justice causes, and the fight against organ harvesting is no exception. Christian organizations and churches often engage in awareness campaigns, support victims, and advocate for ethical organ donation practices. They work not only to combat the illegal trade but also to foster a culture of altruism and voluntary organ donation, in line with ethical and moral principles.

For example, various Christian health organizations actively promote ethical organ donation, ensuring that donations are made freely and without coercion or financial incentive. They educate communities about the need for organ donation while upholding the dignity and value of every human life.

In conclusion, the Christian perspective on organ harvesting is deeply rooted in the teachings of scripture and the life of Jesus Christ. It emphasizes the sanctity of human life, the dignity of the human body, and the moral imperative to protect the vulnerable. Christians are called to be a voice for the voiceless, standing against the atrocities of organ harvesting and trafficking.

This narrative, interweaving Christian teachings and perspectives, adds another layer to the complex tapestry of the global fight against organ trafficking. It calls for compassion, justice, and active engagement in safeguarding the dignity and sanctity of every human being, in line with the profound teachings of Christianity.

From Victims to Advocates

In the saga of combating human trafficking, particularly organ trafficking, a multifaceted approach is necessary—one that encompasses not just the criminal justice system but also focuses on survivor healing and prevention. This narrative, enriched by insights from the Urban Institute's research, unveils the complex layers of justice as perceived by survivors of human trafficking and the stakeholders within the justice system.

The story begins with the voices of survivors, crucial yet often overlooked in the discourse of justice. The Urban Institute's research illuminates that more than three-quarters of survivors do not equate justice with the incarceration of their traffickers. Instead, their notion of justice transcends the conventional punitive measures. It is more about halting the cycle of trafficking and ensuring that no one else endures similar suffering.

For survivors, justice is deeply intertwined with personal healing, autonomy, and empowerment. The research reveals that they see personal stability and access to resources as fundamental in achieving a sense of liberation. This perspective challenges the traditional narrative of justice, steering it towards a more holistic and victim-centric approach.

Contrasting with the survivors, stakeholders in the justice system, including law enforcement officers and prosecutors, maintain a more conventional view of justice. They prioritize criminal prosecution of traffickers, focusing on account-ability and legal retribution. However, there is a growing recognition of the need to align legal out-comes with survivors' needs and well-being.

Models of Justice

The narrative delves into three alternative models of justice that could reshape the landscape of trafficking justice:

1. **Procedural Justice**: This model under-scores the importance of fairness in the processes that resolve disputes. It empha-sizes the involvement of victims in the justice process, allowing them to narrate their stories and influence decisions af-fecting them.

2. **Restorative Justice**: Restorative justice focuses on repairing the harm caused by crime. It brings together victims, of-fenders, and communities to decide on the course of action, which may include

acknowledgment of wrongdoing, apologies, confrontation opportunities, and reparations.

3. **Transitional Justice**: Transitional justice is about community-wide responses to crimes like trafficking. It involves acknowledging harms, preventing recurrence, and includes reforms, education, and public awareness efforts.

Recommendations for a Refined Approach

The Urban Institute's research offers valuable recommendations for a more compassionate and effective approach to trafficking justice:

- Adoption of a trauma-informed, respectful treatment approach by law enforcement.

- Diversification of law enforcement to better represent vulnerable populations.

- Enhanced training for criminal justice actors on trafficking identification, response, and survivor respect.

- Decriminalization of survivors and the incorporation of alternative forms of justice.

- Investment in prevention and rehabilitation programs for traffickers.

- Improved monitoring of incarcerated traffickers to prevent ongoing criminal activities.

Conclusion: A Paradigm Shift in Trafficking Justice

The narrative concludes that trafficking justice is not a one-dimensional concept confined to legal prosecution. It is a multifaceted entity where the survivor's healing, empowerment, and autonomy are as crucial as the legal consequences for traffickers. The alternative models of justice—procedural, restorative, and transitional—offer pathways to a more survivor-centered approach, aligning legal processes with the needs and healing of survivors. This holistic approach to justice not only seeks to punish the perpetrators but also to heal the victims and prevent future occurrences of such crimes.

In the fight against human trafficking, particularly organ trafficking, embracing this nuanced understanding of justice could lead to more effective and compassionate outcomes, truly serving the needs of survivors while holding traffickers accountable. This saga of organ trafficking and the quest for justice calls for a paradigm shift—a move towards a more inclusive, empathetic, and holistic approach to justice. As we journey further into the heart of the organ trafficking crisis, it becomes clear that this is not merely a legal issue, but a profound human tragedy that calls for a holistic response. The narrative now explores the deeper societal and ethical implications of organ trafficking, examining the roles of various stakeholders in this complex issue.

Societal Implications

The impact of organ trafficking extends beyond individual victims and perpetrators, affecting society at large. It raises serious ethical concerns and challenges our collective moral compass. The desperation of those in need of organs, the vulnerability of the exploited donors, and the involvement of healthcare professionals and other intermediaries in this illegal trade paint a disturbing picture of societal imbalances and injustices.

This part of the story brings to light the harsh realities faced by the donors, often driven by extreme poverty and lack of opportunities. Their exploitation is a stark reminder of the socio-economic inequalities that plague our world. The narrative emphasizes the need for broader social reforms to address the root causes of such exploitation, including poverty alleviation, education, and improved healthcare access.

The saga also delves into the ethical dilemmas faced by healthcare professionals. While the medical community is bound by ethical codes and the principle of "do no harm," the covert nature of organ trafficking often puts them in challenging positions. The narrative examines the fine line between complicity and ignorance, emphasizing the need for stricter regulations and ethical guidelines in the medical field to prevent the exploitation of vulnerable individuals for organ trafficking.

In response to this global crisis, international cooperation and policy reforms emerge as critical themes. The narrative highlights the efforts of governments, international organizations, and non-governmental organizations in crafting policies and strategies to combat organ trafficking. It underscores the importance of international treaties, collaborative law enforcement efforts, and comprehensive legal frameworks to effectively address this transnational issue.

Examples of successful international collaborations and policy reforms are woven into the story, showcasing how collective action can lead to significant progress in the fight against organ trafficking. These examples serve as beacons of hope, demonstrating that change is possible with concerted effort and cooperation.

The Role of Education and Awareness

Education and awareness are identified as powerful tools in combating organ trafficking. The narrative emphasizes the importance of public awareness campaigns, education programs, and community outreach initiatives to inform and empower individuals. By raising awareness about the realities of organ trafficking, its signs, and the ethical implications, these initiatives can play a crucial role in prevention and early intervention.

Survivors' Stories: From Victims to Advocates

The narrative also pays tribute to the survivors of organ trafficking, whose stories are not just tales of victimhood but also powerful testimonies of resilience and advocacy. These survivors often become the most passionate and effective advocates for change, using their experiences to raise awareness, support other victims, and lobby for policy reforms. Their stories are woven throughout the narrative, adding a deeply personal and human dimension to the issue.

In exploring the Christian perspective on the atrocities of organ harvesting, human trafficking, and related forms of exploitation, scriptures and parables play a pivotal role in shaping the ethical and moral framework against such injustices. The book of Amos, with its powerful call for justice and righteousness, sets the tone for this examination.In the book of Amos, chapter 5, verses 21-24, God's words, spoken through the ancient prophet, continue to resonate today:

"Even though you offer me your burnt offerings

and grain offerings,

I will not accept them;

and the offerings of well-being of your fatted ani-

mals

I will not look upon.

Take away from me the noise of your songs;

I will not listen to the melody of your harps.

But let justice roll down like waters,

and righteousness like an ever-flowing stream."

Scriptural Insights on Justice and Human Dignity

1. **Micah 6:8**: "He has told you, O mortal, what is good; and what does the Lord require of you but to do justice, and to love kindness, and to walk humbly with your God?" This verse encapsulates the Christian ethos of justice and compassion, underscoring the responsibility to act against injustice and exploitation, such as human trafficking and organ har-

vesting.

2. **Proverbs 31:8-9**: "Speak up for those who cannot speak for themselves, for the rights of all who are destitute. Speak up and judge fairly; defend the rights of the poor and needy." This passage calls Christians to be advocates for the voiceless and marginalized, including victims of trafficking and exploitation.

3. **Luke 10:25-37 - The Parable of the Good Samaritan**: This parable teaches the importance of compassion and assistance for those who are suffering and in need. It challenges individuals to take action against atrocities like human trafficking, emphasizing the duty to care for those who are victimized and vulnerable.

4. **Matthew 25:35-40**: In this passage, Jesus speaks of serving those in need, stat-

ing, "Whatever you did for one of the least of these brothers and sisters of mine, you did for me." This scripture encourages Christians to see serving and protecting victims of trafficking and exploitation as serving Christ Himself.

5. **Isaiah 1:17**: "Learn to do good; seek justice, correct oppression; bring justice to the fatherless, plead the widow's cause." This verse urges believers to actively pursue justice and confront oppression, resonating deeply with the fight against human trafficking.

Parables and Christian Teachings Against Exploitation

1. **The Parable of the Sheep and the Goats (Matthew 25:31-46)**: This parable emphasizes caring for those in need as a fundamental Christian duty. It speaks

against the indifference that often characterizes societal attitudes toward human trafficking and exploitation.

2. **Teachings of Jesus on Loving One's Neighbor (Mark 12:31)**: This core Christian teaching urges believers to love their neighbors as themselves, a directive that inherently opposes any form of exploitation or dehumanization found in human trafficking and organ harvesting.

3. **The Parable of the Rich Man and Lazarus (Luke 16:19-31)**: This story highlights the consequences of ignoring the suffering of others. It serves as a moral lesson on the importance of compassion and empathy for those who are suffering, including victims of trafficking and exploitation.

Conclusion: A Christian Response to Atrocities

From a Christian perspective, responding to the horrors of human trafficking, organ harvesting, and debt bondage requires more than mere recognition of the issues. It demands active engagement in justice and mercy, grounded in the teachings and parables of the Bible. Christians are called to be advocates for the oppressed, to provide support and care for the victims, and to work tirelessly towards eradicating these forms of modern-day slavery.

This narrative, rooted in scriptural guidance and the life of Jesus Christ, reinforces the belief that every human being is made in the image of God and deserves to live a life free from exploitation and injustice. It is a call to the Christian community to embody the principles of justice, mercy, and love in tangible actions against these grave injustices.

The saga of organ trafficking is a call for collective action and a shared moral responsibility. It is a challenge to confront the uncomfortable truths of this hidden trade and work towards a future where such exploitation is unthinkable. The narrative concludes with a powerful call to governments, the medical community, civil society, and individuals to join forces in a unified response to end organ trafficking.

This story of organ trafficking, with its complex layers of legal, ethical, and societal issues, is a sobering reminder of the work that remains to be done. It is an invitation to each of us to play a part in this global fight, contributing to a world where human dignity and justice prevail over greed and exploitation.

"Echoes of Wilberforce:

"Echoes of Wilberforce: A Modern Crusade for Freedom" is a narrative that weaves together the historic fight against slavery led by William Wilberforce with contemporary efforts against modern slavery. It's a story that resonates with the timeless struggle for freedom, justice, and the inherent dignity of all human beings.

In the quiet halls of history, the echoes of a past battle against the atrocity of slavery resonate, blending seamlessly into the present. The narrative begins with William Wilberforce, a figure of the early 19th century, whose impassioned words still stir the soul: "You may choose to look the other way but you can never say again that you did not know."

Wilberforce, a devout Christian and British politician, was a beacon of hope in a world darkened by the slave trade. His determination, as he once declared, "never to rest till I affected its abolition!" set the foundation for a legacy that transcends time. His fight was not just a political one; it was a spiritual crusade, grounded in the belief in the inherent worth and dignity of all human beings, echoing the principles of 1 John 4:20 and Galatians 3:28.

Fast forward to the present day, where the battle against modern slavery rages on. In a small community center, a group of activists gathers, each inspired by Wilberforce's legacy. Among them is Michael, a young man whose resolve is fueled by the teachings of Jesus Christ and the words of

Galatians 3:28, calling for the acceptance of all as equals in Christ.

As the group discusses strategies to combat modern slavery, they reflect on Wilberforce's strategies and his unwavering faith. They draw parallels between the historical context of the 19th century and today's fight against human trafficking and exploitation. "Wilberforce's battle was not in vain," Michael asserts, "for it is upon his legacy that we build our fight."

The narrative delves into the moralistic underpinnings of their crusade. They understand that to combat modern slavery, they must not only address the physical chains but also the metaphysical bonds of prejudice and ignorance. They recognize that their mission is deeply rooted in Christian values, a call to see beyond race, gender, and nationality, as Jesus taught.

The group organizes a series of events, mirroring the efforts of the Society for Effecting the Abolition of the Slave Trade. They gather evidence, share stories, and lobby for change, just as Wilberforce and his contemporaries did. In a poignant scene, they host a vigil, where the powerful words of Wilberforce are recited, reminding them of the long journey from awareness to action.

As the chapter progresses, the story of Wilberforce's tireless campaign in Parliament unfolds, highlighting his 20-year struggle leading to the 1807 Abolition of the Slave Trade Act. The activists draw strength from his perseverance, understanding that their journey, too, might be long and fraught with challenges.

The narrative culminates in a powerful call to action, echoing the urgency of 2 Corinthians 5:20. The group, now more determined than ever, vows to continue their crusade against modern slavery, inspired by the historical abolitionist movement and guided by their faith.

The saga concludes with a reflection on the transformative power of faith and action. Just as Wilberforce's faith guided him to change the course of history, the group realizes that their faith can be the catalyst for modern change. They understand that the battle against slavery, past and present, is not just a physical fight but a metaphysical journey towards a world where love, acceptance, and justice prevail.As the chapter continues, the narrative expands, further intertwining the philosophical and spiritual essence of the historic abolition movement with the ongoing crusade against modern slavery. The story, grounded in metaphysical analysis, dives deeper into the complexities of this moral struggle.

In a church basement, a diverse group of faith leaders and activists gather, inspired by the Interfaith Human Trafficking Toolkit. They represent a spectrum of beliefs – Christians, Muslims, Jews, Buddhists, Bahá'ís, and more – each bringing unique insights but united in a common purpose. The meeting, initiated by Michael, is a melting pot of ideas and strategies to tackle human trafficking.

As they delve into the Toolkit, they find it to be a treasure trove of wisdom and practical guidance. It offers not only a deeper understanding of human trafficking but also empowers them with faith-based resources and action ideas. They discuss the connection between consumerism and trafficking, realizing how everyday choices can inadvertently fuel this global crisis.

The group is particularly moved by the section on children's vulnerability to trafficking. They resolve to focus their efforts on educating and protecting the youth in their communities. As they share prayers and scriptures from their respective faiths, a powerful sense of unity and determination fills the room.

Emma, drawing inspiration from the Toolkit, proposes an interfaith awareness campaign. She envisions a series of events that not only educate but also inspire action across different communities. The campaign would utilize the resources from the Toolkit, tailoring them to resonate with each faith group's unique practices and beliefs.

Michael, reflecting on Wilberforce's legacy, sees a parallel in their efforts. Just as Wilberforce used his faith and parliamentary platform to bring about change, they too can use their diverse platforms to advocate for the victims of modern slavery. He quotes Wilberforce, "so enormous, so dreadful, so irredeemable did (slavery's) wickedness appear," emphasizing the moral imperative of their mission.

The narrative then shifts to a series of community events organized by the group. Each event is tailored to a different faith community, yet the message is universal – a call to action against the scourge of human trafficking. The events are a blend of education, prayer, and discussion, creating a space for understanding and collaboration.

In one poignant scene, a survivor of trafficking shares her story at a joint faith gathering. Her testimony, raw and powerful, serves as a stark reminder of the reality of modern slavery. It galvanizes the group, reaffirming their commitment to the cause.

As the evening draws to a close, the group reflects on their journey. They recognize that their fight against modern slavery is more than a physical struggle; it is a metaphysical journey, a battle against apathy, greed, and moral decay. Their diverse faith perspectives provide a rich tapestry of moral and spiritual guidance, fueling their mission.

The nights training,concludes with a renewed sense of hope and purpose. The group, inspired by the Toolkit and the legacy of Wilberforce, is more united than ever. They understand that their collective efforts, rooted in faith and driven by compassion, can make a profound impact in the fight against modern slavery.

In a world where the echoes of history still resonate, where the battles for freedom are fought on the battlegrounds of faith, love, and courage, this is a story that intertwines the past and the present. Inspired by the unwavering spirit of giants like Wilberforce and Tubman, it serves as a powerful reminder that the fight for liberation is far from over. With resilience as their armor and hope as their guiding light, our protagonists embark on a journey that unveils the true meaning of freedom—a world where every soul is cherished, honored, and unshackled.

Slavery in the 18th and 19th centuries is different than what is becoming a major international human rights form of injustice that violates each victim's God-given value as human beings. With the work of the slavery abolitionists making the sale of another human a crime, it leaves only criminals to be the perpetrators. Protecting people in originating countries is what Christians should find as a priority and bring the force of a unified front by churches, law enforcement, and prosecution leaders. Forced labor, human trafficking, and debt bondage are all forms of modern-day slavery that continue to exist in various parts of the world. Forced labor involves individuals being coerced or forced to work against their will, often under the threat of violence or punishment.

Human trafficking is a grave crime that involves various methods to exploit individuals. It encompasses the recruitment, transportation, transfer, or harboring of people through the use of force, threats, coercion, abduction, fraud, deception, abuse of power, or taking advantage of their vulnerability.

The scourge of human trafficking, particularly in the form of forced labor, represents one of the most heinous violations of human rights in modern society. This explores the dynamics of forced labor, underlining its definition, manifestations, and the urgent need for abolitionist efforts in today's world, drawing from contemporary authors and experts in the field.

Forced labor, a modern incarnation of slavery, is a global epidemic where individuals are coerced into work through deceit, intimidation, or outright violence. This thesis examines the mechanisms of this exploitation and amplifies the call for urgent abolitionist action, as echoed by contemporary authors and human rights advocates.

Forced labor, also known as labor trafficking, is a pernicious form of modern slavery. It involves individuals being compelled to work against their will, often under the guise of debt bondage. Here, victims are deceived into working long hours with little or no pay to repay a debt that may be real or fictitious. Kevin Bales, a leading expert on modern slavery, describes this situation as "new slavery," characterized by psychological manipulation and economic exploitation, in his seminal work, "Disposable People: New Slavery in the Global Economy."

This form of trafficking is not limited to any single industry. It pervades various sectors such as agriculture, manufacturing, construction, and domestic work. For instance, Siddharth Kara, in "Sex Trafficking: Inside the Business of Modern Slavery," highlights cases in industries like textile and garment production, where workers, often women and children, are subjected to inhumane working conditions. They are lured by promises of employment and a better life, only to find themselves entrapped in a cycle of abuse and exploitation.

Moreover, the perpetuation of forced labor is often facilitated by systemic issues such as poverty, lack of education, and inadequate legal protections. As posited by E. Benjamin Skinner in "A Crime So Monstrous: Face-to-Face with Modern-Day Slavery," the root causes of labor trafficking are deeply embedded in societal structures, making the battle against it complex and multifaceted.

In discussing solutions, it is crucial to recognize the role of policy reform and international cooperation. Authors like Louise Shelley in "Human Trafficking: A Global Perspective" emphasize the need for robust legal frameworks and cross-border collaboration to dismantle trafficking networks. Furthermore, the engagement of the public through awareness and education is vital. Gary Haugen and Victor Boutros in "The Locust Effect: Why the End of Poverty Requires the End of Violence," argue for a grassroots approach, empowering local communities to recognize and combat instances of forced labor.

Examples and Quotes

1. **Agriculture**: In "Disposable People," Kevin Bales notes, "In agricultural slavery, people are treated as chattel - a piece of property that can be bought, used, and disposed of."

2. **Manufacturing**: Siddharth Kara's analysis in "Sex Trafficking" reveals, "In sweatshops across the globe, the dreams of the destitute are converted into high fashion nightmares."

3. **Domestic Work**: Skinner, in "A Crime So Monstrous," recounts, "Many domestic workers find themselves in a private prison, where the abuse is unseen and their voices unheard."

The fight against forced labor requires a multifaceted approach that includes legal action, international cooperation, and grassroots mobilization. As these modern authors elucidate, the abolitionist movement needs to adapt to the complexities of contemporary society, targeting the root causes and manifestations of labor trafficking. The collective effort to end this form of modern slavery is not just a legal or economic challenge, but a moral imperative, as underscored by the profound insights and calls to action from these leading voices in the fight against human trafficking.

The global crisis of human trafficking, encompassing forced labor, sexual exploitation, and organ trafficking, represents a severe violation of human dignity and rights. This thesis delves into the intricacies of human trafficking, reflecting on the perspectives and insights from modern authors who emphasize the need for abolitionist efforts in our society.

Human trafficking, a grave human rights violation, involves the illegal trade and exploitation of vulnerable individuals for forced labor, sexual exploitation, or organ trafficking. This thesis explores the dimensions of this global issue, drawing on contemporary authors' insights to underscore the urgent need for comprehensive and collaborative abolitionist strategies.

Human trafficking is characterized by the recruitment, transportation, and exploitation of people through deception, coercion, or violence. Victims, often children, refugees, and migrants, are trapped in a cycle of abuse and exploitation. In her book "Walking Prey: How America's Youth are Vulnerable to Sex Slavery," Holly Austin Smith highlights the susceptibility of young individuals to trafficking, emphasizing the role of societal factors in their victimization.

The scope of human trafficking is vast, encompassing forced labor in industries like agriculture and manufacturing, sexual exploitation in the form of prostitution or pornography, and even the illicit trade of human organs. Louise Shelley, in "Human Trafficking: A Global Perspective," discusses the multifaceted nature of trafficking networks and their operation across international borders, emphasizing the complexity of combating this global scourge.

Authors such as Siddharth Kara in "Sex Trafficking: Inside the Business of Modern Slavery" shed light on the economic dynamics underpinning human trafficking, particularly the immense profits generated at the expense of victims' freedom and well-being. Kara's research underscores the need for a concerted effort to dismantle the economic incentives driving traffickers.

Kevin Bales, in "Disposable People: New Slavery in the Global Economy," further discusses the dehumanization of victims in the trafficking trade. He emphasizes that understanding the mindset and methods of traffickers is crucial in developing effective abolitionist strategies.

Examples and Quotes

1. **Sexual Exploitation**: As Holly Austin Smith writes in "Walking Prey," "Sex traf-

ficking thrives in a society where women and children are objectified and commodified."

2. **Forced Labor**: Siddharth Kara, in "Sex Trafficking," notes, "The global economy's insatiable demand for cheap labor fuels the fire of trafficking in the labor sector."

3. **Organ Trafficking**: Shelley, in "Human Trafficking," reveals, "The clandestine nature of organ trafficking makes it one of the most challenging forms of trafficking to combat."

Combating human trafficking requires a comprehensive approach that encompasses legal, social, and economic strategies. As highlighted by modern authors, the abolitionist movement must focus on understanding the multi-dimensional nature of trafficking, addressing the root causes, and providing support and empowerment to victims. This fight against human trafficking is not only a legal battle but also a moral imperative, calling for the collective effort of governments, organizations, and individuals worldwide. The insights from these authors serve as a powerful reminder of the urgency and necessity of global collaboration in eradicating this heinous crime against humanity.

Debt bondage, a sinister form of modern slavery, is particularly rampant in South Asia and other regions, trapping individuals in a vicious cycle of debt and forced labor. In this thesis, I will explore the phenomenon of debt bondage, incorporating examples and quotes from contemporary authors who address the need for abolitionist efforts to eradicate this scourge.

Debt bondage, a modern form of slavery, forces individuals to work off debts under exploitative conditions, often perpetuated through inflated debts and unending servitude. This thesis examines the nature of debt bondage, its prevalence in various industries, and the voices of modern authors advocating for its abolition.

Debt bondage occurs when individuals are compelled to work to repay a debt, often inherited or incurred through deception. The terms of repayment are usually exploitative, with victims working in harsh conditions for little or no pay. Siddharth Kara, in his book "Bonded Labor: Tackling the System of Slavery in South Asia," provides an in-depth analysis of how debt bondage is perpetuated through manipulated debts and exorbitant interest rates, making it nearly impossible for victims to escape.

Kevin Bales, in "Disposable People: New Slavery in the Global Economy," highlights the insidious nature of debt bondage, where the debt often becomes a tool for control and exploitation. He points out that victims are not only physically restrained but are also psychologically bound by the debt they owe.

Louise Shelley, in "Human Trafficking: A Global Perspective," emphasizes that debt bondage is not restricted to any single industry. It is prevalent in agriculture, manufacturing, mining, and other sectors, where workers are subjected to long hours of labor with little hope of repaying their debts.

The cycle of debt bondage is further complicated by threats of violence or legal action, as noted by E. Benjamin Skinner in "A Crime So Monstrous: Face-to-Face with Modern-Day Slavery." He describes how victims, often from marginalized communities, are trapped in a system that devalues their labor and dignity.

Examples and Quotes

1. **Agriculture**: Siddharth Kara, in "Bond-

ed Labor," notes, "In the agricultural sector, bonded laborers work from dawn to dusk, yet their debts only seem to grow, not diminish."

2. **Manufacturing**: Kevin Bales observes in "Disposable People," "In factories, the debt bondage system ensures a compliant and cheap workforce, hidden from the eyes of the law."

3. **Mining**: Louise Shelley highlights in "Human Trafficking," "The mining industry exploits debt bondage, trapping workers in dangerous conditions with the false promise of freedom."

Addressing debt bondage requires a multi-faceted approach, involving legal, economic, and social interventions. The insights from modern authors underline the need for stronger laws, better enforcement, and more awareness to prevent exploitation. They also emphasize the importance of empowering victims and providing them with viable alternatives to escape the bondage. The abolition of debt bondage is not just a legal imperative but a moral one, demanding the collective effort of governments, NGOs, and civil society. The voices of these authors serve as a clarion call for action against this form of modern slavery, urging us to dismantle the structures that perpetuate debt bondage and restore dignity and freedom to its victims.

The Coalition of Catholic Organizations Against Human Trafficking

In the realm of religious leaders who have spoken out against slavery and modern forms of human trafficking, Catholic figures have played a significant role. Their voices have echoed with a resounding call for justice, compassion, and the recognition of the inherent dignity of every human being.

Pope Francis, the spiritual leader of the Catholic Church, has been at the forefront of this movement. In a powerful statement delivered on November 7, 2016, during the RENATE Conference (Religious in Europe Networking Against Trafficking and Exploitation), he addressed the issue head-on. He stated, "One of the most troubling of those open wounds (in the world) is the trade in human beings, a modern form of slavery. It violates the God-given dignity of so many of our brothers and sisters and constitutes a true crime against humanity."

These words encapsulate the gravity of the situation and the urgency to combat human trafficking. The Pope's statement not only acknowledges the existence of this heinous crime but also emphasizes the moral obligation to protect the vulnerable and restore their dignity.

Catholic authors have also contributed to the

discourse against slavery and human trafficking. Their writings have served as a source of inspiration and enlightenment, shedding light on the dark corners of this global issue. For instance, renowned Catholic author and theologian, Henri Nouwen, in his book "The Wounded Healer," delves into the depths of human suffering and advocates for a compassionate response to those affected by slavery and exploitation.

Nouwen writes, "To speak about the woundedness of our world, to speak about the pain of our world, to speak about the suffering of our world, is not a sign of weakness but a sign of strength." These words remind us that acknowledging the existence of human trafficking and standing against it requires courage and a commitment to justice.

Another influential Catholic author, Dorothy Day, co-founder of the Catholic Worker Movement, dedicated her life to serving the poor and marginalized. In her autobiography, "The Long Loneliness," she reflects on the interconnectedness of social justice and the fight against slavery. She writes, "We cannot love God unless we love each other, and to love we must know each other. We know Him in the breaking of bread, and we know each other in the breaking of bread, and we are not alone anymore."

Day's words highlight the importance of solidarity and community in combating the dehumanizing effects of slavery and human trafficking. They remind us that it is through genuine human connection and empathy that we can truly understand the suffering of others and work towards their liberation.

The Catholic Church's stance against slavery and human trafficking is rooted in its core teachings of love, justice, and the inherent dignity of every human person. Through the words of Pope Francis and the writings of Catholic authors like Henri Nouwen and Dorothy Day, we are reminded of our collective responsibility to fight against this modern-day form of slavery and to restore the dignity of those who have been victimized.

In conclusion, the Catholic Church, through the voices of its religious leaders and authors, has spoken out against slavery and human trafficking with a compelling blend of intrigue, compassion, suspense, and informative insights. Their words serve as a call to action, urging us to join the fight against this grave injustice and to work towards a world where every individual is free and their dignity is respected.

Scripture

•Genesis 1:27 "...in the image of God they were created; male and female God created them."

• Matthew 25:35-40 "Whatever you did to one of the least of these, you did to me..."

• Matthew 19:13-15 "...Jesus said, 'Let the little children come to me and do not hinder them, for to such belongs the kingdom of heaven'."

• Mark 12:31 "...You shall love your neighbor as yourself."

• 1 Corinthians 3:16 "...the Spirit of God dwells in you."

• Galatians 3:28: "There is neither Jew nor Greek, slave nor free..."

The Coalition of Catholic Organizations Against Human Trafficking (CCOAHT) is a collective of national and international Catholic agencies dedicated to eradicating the abhorrent practice of human trafficking. The Coalition has several key objectives:

1. Developing comprehensive strategies to combat trafficking and support its victims.

2. Promoting the establishment of services for trafficking survivors and empowering them to rebuild their lives.

3. Engaging in dialogue with government officials and other stakeholders involved in shaping public policies related to human trafficking.

4. Devising effective approaches for public education, awareness-raising, and grassroots activism.

With over 30 member organizations, the Coalition of Catholic Organizations Against Human Trafficking has extensive networks of passionate individuals committed to eliminating human trafficking. These organizations contribute to the fight against trafficking through various initiatives, including:

1. Providing safe havens for trafficked adolescents and adults within the United States.

2. Offering direct services to adult and child trafficking victims both domestically and internationally.

3. Implementing prevention projects in regions such as Eastern Europe, India, and Latin America.

4. Delivering national training and technical assistance on the issue of trafficking.

5. Engaging in meetings with government officials, including Senators, Representatives in the U.S. Congress, and representatives from the U.S. State Department's Office to Monitor & Combat Trafficking in Persons, the Department of Health & Human Services, and the Department of Justice.

In the book of Amos, chapter 5, verses 21-24, God's words, spoken through the ancient prophet, continue to resonate today:

"Even though you offer me your burnt offerings and grain offerings,
I will not accept them;
and the offerings of well-being of your fatted animals
I will not look upon.
Take away from me the noise of your songs;

I will not listen to the melody of your harps.
But let justice roll down like waters,
and righteousness like an ever-flowing stream."

These powerful words remind us of the importance of pursuing justice and righteousness in all aspects of our lives.

In Exodus 14:10, 11, 13-15, 19-22, we witness the story of the Israelites' escape from slavery in Egypt. When faced with the pursuing Egyptians and seemingly insurmountable obstacles, Moses reassures the people, saying, "Fear not, stand firm, and see the salvation of the Lord, which he will work for you today." Through divine intervention, the Lord parts the Red Sea, allowing the Israelites to pass through on dry ground, symbolizing liberation from bondage.

These biblical passages serve as powerful reminders of God's call for justice, freedom, and the liberation of all people from oppression. They inspire us to take action against modern-day forms of slavery, such as human trafficking.

In addition to these scriptures, Catholic religious leaders have also spoken out against slavery and human trafficking. Their words serve as guiding principles for the fight against these injustices. Here are a few quotes from Catholic religious leaders:

1. Pope Francis: "Human trafficking is an open wound on the body of contemporary society, a scourge upon the body of Christ. It is a crime against humanity."

2. Saint John Paul II: "The trade in human beings constitutes a shocking offense against human dignity and a grave violation of fundamental human rights."

3. Saint Oscar Romero: "We must not seek the child Jesus in the pretty figures of our Christmas cribs. We must seek him among the undernourished children who have gone to bed at night with nothing to eat, among the poor newsboys who will sleep covered with newspapers in doorways."

As we delve deeper into the Christian perspective on the atrocities of organ harvesting, sex trafficking, and debt bondage, it becomes evident that these practices are fundamentally at odds with the core teachings of Christianity. The scripture from Amos 5:21-24 is a powerful denunciation of empty rituals and a call for genuine justice and righteousness. This narrative explores several more scriptures and parables that embody the essence of Christian anti-human trafficking beliefs, emphasizing the sanctity of human life and the imperative to protect the vulnerable.

Scriptures Condemning Exploitation and Injustice

1. **Proverbs 31:8-9**: "Speak up for those

who cannot speak for themselves, for the rights of all who are destitute. Speak up and judge fairly; defend the rights of the poor and needy." This passage calls Christians to be advocates for those who are voiceless and oppressed, a mandate that directly relates to victims of human trafficking and organ harvesting.

2. **Isaiah 1:17**: "Learn to do right; seek justice. Defend the oppressed. Take up the cause of the fatherless; plead the case of the widow." Isaiah urges the faithful to actively seek justice and defend those who are oppressed, a clear directive against practices like human trafficking that prey on the vulnerable.

3. **Matthew 25:35-40**: In this passage, Jesus talks about caring for the needy - "I was hungry and you gave me something

to eat, I was thirsty and you gave me something to drink, I was a stranger and you invited me in." This teaching of Christ emphasizes the importance of compassion and action in response to human suffering, principles fundamentally violated by human trafficking and organ harvesting.

Parables and Teachings Against Exploitation

1. **The Parable of the Good Samaritan (Luke 10:25-37)**: This well-known parable tells of a Samaritan who helps a man beaten and left for dead, while others pass by. It exemplifies the call to love and care for one's neighbor, regardless of their background or circumstances. In the context of human trafficking and organ harvesting, this parable speaks to the responsibility of Christians to aid those who are exploited and abused.

2. **The Parable of the Sheep and the Goats (Matthew 25:31-46)**: In this parable, Jesus separates the righteous from the unrighteous based on their actions towards the needy, saying, "Whatever you did for one of the least of these brothers and sisters of mine, you did for me." This teaching underscores the Christian duty to protect and support the vulnerable, a principle starkly violated by the dehumanizing nature of trafficking and forced organ harvesting.

Christian Advocacy and Action Against Trafficking

Inspired by these scriptures and teachings, many Christian organizations and churches actively participate in combating human trafficking and organ harvesting. They engage in awareness campaigns, support survivors, and advocate for ethical practices and policies. For example, initiatives like The A21 Campaign and International Justice Mission work globally to rescue victims, prosecute traffickers, and strengthen legal systems.

Conclusion: A Call to Righteous Action

In conclusion, the Christian perspective on the atrocities of human trafficking, including organ harvesting and sex trafficking, is deeply rooted in the Bible's teachings about justice, compassion, and the value of every human life. The scriptures and parables discussed here call Christians to actively oppose these injustices and to be a voice for the oppressed. They serve as a moral compass guiding the faithful to not only denounce such atrocities but also to take tangible actions to aid victims and prevent future exploitation. This narrative is a reminder that in the Christian faith, true worship is not just about rituals or songs, but about letting "justice roll down like waters, and righteousness like an ever-flowing stream."

These quotes and scriptures remind us of the urgent need to combat human trafficking and slavery, and they inspire us to work towards a world where justice, freedom, and dignity are upheld for all.

Prayer Resources • The Beatitudes: A Contemporary Version, composed by the International Sisters of Mercy Global Action Opposing Human Trafficking Working Group, February 2015. • A Prayer to End Human Trafficking, Sisters of Charity of Saint Elizabeth, Convent Station, NJ: prayer card in several languages. • See several prayer resources on the website of the Intercommunity Peace & Justice Center, Seattle, WA.

Educational Resources • The Catholic Health Association offers many valuable resources to assist health care organizations and health care professionals to identify and assist victims of human trafficking. • The USCCB Anti-Trafficking Program educates about human trafficking as an offense against the fundamental dignity of the human person and provides training and technical assistance on this issue. • U.S. Catholic Sisters Against Human Trafficking offers educational modules on many human trafficking topics including: Human Trafficking and the Objectification of Women; Reducing the Demand for Human Trafficking; Human Trafficking & Pornography; Human Trafficking for the Purpose of Organ Removal. • The Stop Trafficking newsletter serves as a forum for exchange among religious congregations and their collaborating organizations to promote awareness about human trafficking. • Against Humanity is a project of the Center of Concern which strives to inform the public about the realities of human trafficking and to provide resources for educating and acting in the fight against this terrible scourge.

Excerpts on Slavery and Trafficking from the Bahá'í Sacred Writings

The Bahá'í Sacred Writings encompass a vast body of texts that form the core of the Bahá'í Faith, a monotheistic religion founded in the 19th century by Bahá'u'lláh in Persia. These writings, primarily penned by Bahá'u'lláh himself, are supplemented by texts from his predecessor, the Báb, and elaborations by his son, 'Abdu'l-Bahá. Collectively, they articulate the

Bahá'í teachings and laws, offering guidance on spiritual, moral, and societal issues.

Central to these writings is the Kitáb-i-Aqdas, or "The Most Holy Book," which Bahá'u'lláh revealed as the cornerstone of Bahá'í law. It sets forth the principles of individual conduct and governance, emphasizing the unity of humanity, the importance of education, and the need for global peace and justice. Another significant text is the Kitáb-i-Íqán, or "The Book of Certitude," which provides a theological framework for understanding the succession of divine messengers and the nature of religious truth.

The Bahá'í writings also include numerous tablets and epistles addressing various topics, such as the harmony of science and religion, gender equality, the eradication of prejudice, and the development of a world civilization. The Hidden Words, a collection of short, aphoristic statements, offers spiritual and ethical guidance, distilling the essence of religious teachings.

These texts are not only theological but also poetic and philosophical, blending mystical elements with practical directives. They aim to inspire individuals to transform their lives and society, fostering an ethos of unity, service, and progress. The Bahá'í Sacred Writings are dynamic and evolving, reflecting the faith's belief in progressive revelation and its vision of an ever-advancing civilizat ion.**BAHÁ'Í**

"It is forbidden you to trade in slaves, be they men or women. It is not for him who is himself a servant to buy another of God's servants, and this hath been prohibited in His Holy Tablet. Thus, by His mercy, hath the commandment been recorded by the Pen of justice. Let no man exalt himself above another; all are but bondslaves before the Lord, and all exemplify the truth that there is none other God but Him. He, verily, is the All-Wise, Whose wisdom encompasseth all things."

~ Bahá'u'lláh

"We have been informed that thou hast forbidden the trading in slaves, both men and women. This, verily, is what God hath enjoined in this wondrous Revelation. God hath, truly, destined a reward for thee, because of this. He, verily, will pay the doer of good his due recompense, wert thou to follow what hath been sent unto thee by Him Who is the All-Knowing, the All-Informed."
~ Bahá'u'lláh (in a tablet addressed to Queen Victoria)

"You must show forth that which will be conducive to the welfare and tranquility of the helpless ones of the world. Gird up the loins of effort; perchance the slaves may be emancipated from bondage and find freedom. In this day, the cry of justice is raised and the lamentation of equity is heard."
~ Bahá'u'lláh

"If thine eyes be turned towards mercy, forsake the things that profit thee and cleave unto that which will profit mankind. And if thine eyes be

turned towards justice, choose thou for thy neighbour that which thou choosest for thyself."
~ Bahá'u'lláh

"Blessed is the ruler who succoureth the captive, and the rich one who careth for the poor, and the just one who secureth from the wrong doer the rights of the downtrodden, and happy the trustee who observeth that which the Ordainer, the Ancient of Days hath prescribed unto him."
~ Bahá'u'lláh

"The entire human race are servants of the Lord of might and glory, as He hath brought the whole creation under the purview of His gracious utterance, and hath enjoined upon us to show forth love and affection, wisdom and compassion, faithfulness and unity towards all, without any discrimination."
~ `Abdu'l-Bahá

"Be generous in prosperity, and thankful in adversity. Be worthy of the trust of thy neighbor, and look upon him with a bright and friendly face.

Be a treasure to the poor, an admonisher to the rich, an answerer to the cry of the needy, a preserver of the sanctity of thy pledge. Be fair in thy judgment, and guarded in thy speech. Be unjust to no man, and show all meekness to all men. Be as a lamp unto them that walk in darkness, a joy to the sorrowful, a sea for the thirsty, a haven for the distressed, an upholder and defender of the victim of oppression. Let integrity and uprightness distinguish all thine acts. Be a home for the stranger, a balm to the suffering, a tower of strength for the fugitive. Be eyes to the blind, and a guiding light unto the feet of the erring. Be an ornament to the countenance of truth, a crown to the brow of fidelity, a pillar of the temple of righteousness, a breath of life to the body of mankind, an ensign of the hosts of justice, a luminary above the horizon of virtue, a dew to the soil of the human heart, an ark on the ocean of knowledge, a sun in the heaven of bounty, a gem on the diadem of wisdom, a shining light in the firmament of thy generation, a fruit upon the tree of humility."

~ Bahá'u'lláh

"O CHILDREN OF MEN! Know ye not why We created you all from the same dust? That no one should exalt himself over the other. Ponder at all times in your hearts how ye were created. Since We have created you all from one same substance it is incumbent on you to be even as one soul, to walk with the same feet, eat with the same mouth and dwell in the same land, that from your inmost being, by your deeds and actions, the signs of oneness and the essence of detachment may be made manifest. Such is My counsel to you, O concourse of light! Heed ye this counsel that ye may obtain the fruit of holiness from the tree of wondrous glory."

~ Bahá'u'lláh

"O Thou kind Lord! Thou hast created all humanity from the same stock. Thou hast decreed that all shall belong to the same household. In Thy Holy Presence they are all Thy servants, and all mankind are sheltered beneath Thy Tabernacle; all have gathered together at Thy Table of Bounty; all are illumined through the light of Thy Providence. O God! Thou art kind to all, Thou hast provided for all, dost shelter all, conferrest life upon all. Thou hast endowed each and all with talents and faculties, and all are submerged in the Ocean of Thy Mercy. O Thou kind Lord! Unite all. Let the religions agree and make the nations one, so that they may see each other as one family and the whole earth as one home. May they all live together in perfect harmony. O God! Raise aloft the banner of the oneness of mankind. O God! Establish the Most Great Peace. Cement Thou, O God, the hearts together. O Thou kind Father, God! Gladden our hearts through the fragrance of Thy love. Brighten our eyes through the Light of Thy Guidance. Delight our ears with the melody of Thy Word, and shelter us all in the Stronghold of Thy Providence. Thou art the Mighty and Powerful, Thou art the Forgiving and Thou art the One Who overlooketh the shortcomings of all mankind."

~ `Abdu'l-Bahá

For more information contact the U.S. Bahá'í Office of Public Affairs and its engagement on trafficking and other human rights issues.

"THE CHAINS OF MODERN SLAVERY,":

In the labyrinthine darkness of our modern world, a sinister trade thrives, veiled from the common gaze yet pervasive in its reach. The city's bustling streets, alive with the cacophony of daily life, hide a grim underbelly where human beings are reduced to mere commodities. This is the realm of human trafficking.

Amidst the chaos of the city, unnoticed by the passing throngs, stand the silent victims of this trade. Young women lured by promises of employment, their dreams shattered as they find themselves ensnared in a nightmare of exploitation. Men, driven by the hope of a better life, trapped in endless cycles of forced labor, their sweat and toil lining the pockets of their unseen masters.

The narrative echoes the somber wisdom of Maimonides, the Jewish philosopher, who warned against the complicity in crime by purchasing stolen goods. His words, "One may not buy stolen goods from a thief; to do so is a great transgression," resonate deeply in this context. Human trafficking, in essence, is a theft of lives, a robbery of freedom and dignity.

In one dimly lit corner of the city, a young woman named Sarah huddles in the shadows, a faraway look in her eyes. Once full of hope, she now bears the weight of a reality too cruel to fathom. Sarah's story, like many others, began with a promise – a promise of work, of opportunity.

Instead, she found herself caught in a web from which escape seemed impossible.

Nearby, a young man named David toils under the unrelenting sun, his hands calloused, his spirit broken. Promised a job in construction, he now finds himself a modern-day slave, his every move controlled by those who see him not as a human being, but as an asset to be exploited.

But even in the darkest of nights, there are stars that shine. In this city, there are those who refuse to turn a blind eye to the suffering. Activists, lawyers, and ordinary citizens, armed with compassion and resolve, fight tirelessly to untangle these victims from their chains. They are the beacons of hope in a world that too often seems devoid of it.

The story of Sarah, David, and countless others is a testament to the enduring human spirit, a call to action against the atrocities of human trafficking. It is a narrative that weaves the teachings of Jewish law, the insights of renowned authors, and the practical strategies for combating this global issue into a tapestry of hope and determination.

The notion of human trafficking as a form of theft – the stealing of lives, freedoms, and dignities – is not just a metaphor but a harrowing reality. This chapter unravels the hidden facets of this world, examining the mechanisms and motivations behind this modern form of slavery. It challenges the idea, held by some, that the wealth generated by this inhuman trade could ever justify its existence. In stark contrast, it presents the Jewish religious law as a moral compass, deeming such practices not only unclean but fundamentally against the tenets of justice and humanity.

The narrative begins in the bustling streets of a major city, where the unseen chains of exploitation bind countless souls. Here, we encounter stories of those who have fallen prey to the false promises of traffickers. Their tales are heartbreaking – young women lured by the prospect of employment, only to find themselves trapped in a nightmare of sexual exploitation; men promised work and a new life, only to end up in forced labor with no escape.

As we delve deeper, we find that the roots of this evil trade lie in the very structure of our society. The demand for cheap labor and services, the insatiable appetite for sexual gratification, and the persistent inequalities in wealth and power create fertile ground for human trafficking to flourish. The perpetrators, often shrouded in anonymity, exploit these vulnerabilities with a chilling efficiency.

Yet, in the midst of this darkness, there are beacons of hope. We meet the brave souls who fight against this scourge – activists, lawyers, and ordinary citizens who refuse to turn a blind eye to the suffering around them. They work tirelessly to rescue victims, support survivors, and bring traffickers to justice. Their stories are a testament to the power of human resilience and the enduring spirit of compassion.

To illustrate the gravity of the situation, let's consider some examples. In ancient times, slaves were often captured through wars, raids, or as a result of debt. They were treated as property, bought and sold, and subjected to harsh conditions and abuse. Fast forward to the present day, where human trafficking cartels engage in organized criminal activities, exploiting vulnerable individuals for various purposes such as forced labor, sexual exploitation, or organ trafficking. The methods may have changed, but the underlying cruelty and disregard for human rights persist.

The United Nations recognizes the urgency to address this issue and has taken significant steps to combat human trafficking. Through international cooperation, awareness campaigns, and legal frameworks, they strive to dismantle trafficking networks, protect victims, and prosecute perpetrators. Their efforts reflect a collective desire to overcome illegal trafficking and ensure the freedom and dignity of all individuals.

The historical context of slavery provides valuable insights into our response to modern-day human trafficking. It reminds us that the fight against slavery is an ongoing struggle deeply rooted in our shared history. By standing against oppression and advocating for freedom and dignity, we can work towards a world free from the chains of modern slavery.

In this chapter, we also explore the powerful role of Jewish religious law in combating human trafficking. The teachings of the Torah and the Talmud provide a strong ethical framework that condemns the exploitation of the vulnerable. Jewish law upholds the sanctity of human life and the dignity of every individual, emphasizing the responsibility to protect the weak and oppressed.

Under the flickering fluorescent lights, a diverse group of individuals convenes. Among them are members from the International Labor Organization, the International Organization for Migration, the United Nations Children's Fund, the Office of the United Nations High Commissioner for Human Rights, and the Organization for Security and Cooperation in Europe. They are united by a common goal: to combat the scourge of human trafficking.

The discussion is led by a UN.GIFT representative, who outlines the multifaceted strategy of the initiative. "Our objective," she begins, "is not just to respond to human trafficking, but to anticipate and prevent it. We are here to empower the vulnerable, dismantle the criminal networks, and bring justice to those who exploit human lives."

She elaborates on the nine key objectives of U N.GIFT:

1. **Raising Awareness:** The first step is to shatter the silence surrounding human trafficking. Through campaigns and education, they aim to inform the public about the realities of this trade.

2. **Strengthening Prevention:** Addressing the root causes that make individuals vulnerable to trafficking is crucial. This involves outreach to at-risk groups and alleviating factors like poverty and inequality.

3. **Reducing Demand:** The representative emphasizes the need to target the demand side of human trafficking, reducing the market for exploited labor and services.

4. **Supporting and Protecting Victims:** A comprehensive approach is required to aid victims, including providing housing, counseling, medical care, and considering the special needs of women, children, and at-risk populations like refugees.

5. **Improving Law Enforcement Effectiveness:** Enhancing cooperation between countries to share information on trafficking patterns, trafficker profiles,

and victim identification is key to dismantling criminal networks.

6. **Implementing International Commitments:** The initiative works to turn international agreements into national laws and practices, focusing on countries needing the most support.

7. **Enriching the Database:** A critical aspect is the collection and analysis of data to understand the scope and nature of trafficking better, leading to evidence-based strategies.

8. **Strengthening Partnership:** Building networks involving civil society, intergovernmental organizations, and the private sector is essential for a united front against trafficking.

9. **Ensuring Resources:** Securing sustain-

able funding for anti-trafficking projects worldwide is a priority.

10. **Strengthening Member States' Participation:** Encouraging active participation from Member States is vital for long-term success and ownership of the initiative.

As the meeting progresses, the participants discuss how Jewish law and ethics align with these objectives. Sarah, now a vocal activist, shares her insights. "In Jewish teachings, every individual is of infinite value. The fight against human trafficking is not just a legal battle but a moral imperative," she says passionately.

The narrative then transitions to a more personal level, as Sarah recounts her own harrowing journey from victim to survivor to activist. Her story embodies the pain and resilience of those caught in the web of trafficking, as well as the transformative power of hope and determination.

David, another survivor, speaks of his ordeal and the sense of liberation he experienced upon being rescued. His story is a testament to the effectiveness of coordinated international efforts and the critical role of organizations like UN.GIFT.

"Breaking The Chains of Modern Slavery,":

In "Breaking The Chains of Modern Slavery," a comprehensive examination unravels the intricate workings of human trafficking in contemporary society. This exploration delves deep into the various manifestations of modern enslavement, such as involuntary servitude, sexual coercion, and the burdens of debt bondage, highlighting their prevalence in both developed and less affluent regions. It begins with an incisive analysis of global supply chains, which, often unwittingly, contribute to the perpetuation of such involuntary servitude. Tracing the progression of raw materials like cotton from their origins in plantations to their final form in textile mills, the analysis uncovers the often obscured exploitation inherent in the production of everyday goods. This intricate network of international commerce, vital for economic development, simultaneously acts as a conduit for labor abuses and human trafficking.

This issue resonates deeply with Jewish ethical principles, which emphasize fairness, respect for workers, and the prohibition of oppressing the vulnerable, as taught in foundational texts like Leviticus and Deuteronomy. The modern challenge is to mirror these values in global supply chains. For instance, the cotton industry, a key player in global textiles, has faced scrutiny for labor violations, including forced and child labor, in certain regions. Addressing these concerns requires a multi-pronged approach, combining legal action with a commitment to ethical sourcing and corporate responsibility. Jewish organizations, guided by principles of fairness and dignity for all workers, have been at the forefront of advocating for fair trade and ethical business practices, embodying the Jewish commitment to social justice and tikkun olam, or "repairing the world."

Moreover, recent global assessments reveal a significant number of labor migrants, including those in sectors like textiles in Argentina, gold-mining in Peru, and construction in Kazakhstan, facing extreme exploitation, some identified as victims of trafficking. This groundbreaking research, comparing the experiences of 71 individuals, including both trafficking victims and migrant workers, across various sectors and regions, unveils commonalities in health hazards and challenges faced in different sectors. It highlights the need for policymakers and program staff to consider the broader population of workers in unregulated sectors, as the harms experienced by migrant workers often mirror those of trafficking victims. This call to action urges future interventions to protect against extreme abuses in these informal sectors, aligning with the Jewish ethos of safeguarding every individual's dignity and r ights.Therefore, the struggle against involuntary servitude in global supply chains is not only a legal battle but a moral imperative. It demands a shift in global economic norms towards greater transparency, accountability, and ethical business practices. This aligns with the Jewish ethical framework, advocating for a world where economic growth does not come at the expense of human dignity and rights.

In summary, our journey through the complexities of international supply networks reveals a pressing need to infuse our global economic systems with ethical values and practices. Inspired by Jewish teachings, we are called to action – to reshape our economic landscape in a way that upholds the dignity and rights of every individual involved in the production of the goods we use daily.

Subsequently, we delve into the grim realities of sexual coercion, casting light on the dire circumstances its victims endure. This segment probes the complex lattice of societal elements – poverty, disparity between genders, and systemic corruption – that act as catalysts for this vile crime. In an effort to convey the severity of these conditions, poignant tales of those who have survived such ordeals are presented. These narratives bring a human element to the numbers, emphasizing the critical need for prompt interventions focused on rescue and recovery.

Take, for example, the courageous account of Sarah, who recounts being ensnared by sexual traffickers amidst her family's dire economic plight. Her story vividly depicts how destitution can be a significant driver for such crimes. In a similar vein, Maria's experience uncovers the entrenched gender biases fueling the exploitation of susceptible individuals, marking a clarion call for societal transformation and the empowerment of women.

Moreover, this section casts light on the malignant role of corruption in enabling sexual coercion rings. The transformation of Alex, from a past trafficker to an informant, offers a window into the corrupt systems that sustain these criminal activities. His revelations stress the imperative to dismantle such networks and bring the culprits to justice.

Interlacing these harrowing survival stories and scrutinizing the societal undercurrents, this part of the text emphasizes the pressing need to confront sexual coercion. It advocates for exhaustive recovery and support measures for survivors, alongside tackling the root causes of this atrocious crime.

This discourse intertwines with the Judaic perspective on social justice concerns such as impoverishment, gender disparities, and dishonesty, anchored in the concept of tikkun olam – "mending the world." Jewish thought stresses proactive measures to rectify societal issues, championing fairness and equality.

Within the realm of sexual coercion, numerous Jewish entities and individuals have taken an active role in heightening awareness, aiding survivors, and propelling policy reforms. For instance, the Jewish Coalition Against Sex Trafficking (JCAST) epitomizes a consortium of Jewish groups united in their battle against sexual exploitation and coercion.

A notable instance of Jewish insight on this matter is found in Rabbi Rachel Timoner's advocacies, highlighting the necessity for all-encompassing recovery and support schemes. She accentuates the importance of acknowledging the survivors' humanity and the pressing need for systemic alterations to eradicate the root causes of sexual coercion.

When addressing the predicament of debt servitude, we probe how unethical practices ensnare individuals and families in inescapable debt cycles, perpetuating generations of bondage. This narrative draws parallels with the Judaic stance on usury and the prohibition of exploiting the impoverished, likening it to contemporary predatory lending.

Throughout this segment, we weave together impactful quotes from esteemed writers and sacred texts. These encompass insightful remarks from modern authors spotlighting the plight of those trafficked and enslaved, as well as scriptural references from Judaic sources that highlight the ethical obligations to combat such injustices.

In conclusion, readers are left with an understanding of the immense scale of modern slavery and the diverse strategies necessary to confront it. This chapter calls for a collective effort transcending legal measures, appealing to the moral conscience of communities and the shared duty to preserve human dignity

The Path to Freedom":

from the jewish perspective part three

In "The Path to Freedom," we shift our focus to the solutions and strategies being employed in the fight against human trafficking. This chapter explores how various organizations, governments, and communities are working together to dismantle the structures that allow human trafficking to thrive.

In the vital struggle against human trafficking, the role of interfaith initiatives stands out as a beacon of hope and collaboration. These partnerships, uniting diverse religious communities, leverage their unique perspectives and resources toward a common goal: the eradication of human trafficking. This synergy of faiths is not just about bringing varied viewpoints to the table; it's about uniting in action against a global scourge.

Jewish teachings, deeply rooted in social justice and the protection of the vulnerable, play a critical role in these interfaith efforts. The Jewish concept of tikkun olam, or "repairing the world," aligns perfectly with the mission of these initiatives. It's a call echoed in the words of the Talmud: "Whoever saves a life, it is considered as if they saved an entire world" (Sanhedrin 37a). This principle drives the Jewish community's involvement in collaborative actions to combat human trafficking, emphasizing the sanctity of every human life.

Interfaith programs across the globe have demonstrated significant achievements in rescue operations, providing support to victims, and advocacy. These programs often include faith-based organizations that offer shelter, counseling, and rehabilitation to survivors, guided by their spiritual values and commitment to human dignity. For example, Jewish organizations, alongside Christian, Muslim, and other faith groups, have been instrumental in providing such holistic support, showcasing the power of unity in diversity.

Moving to legislative efforts, the global fight against human trafficking is also being waged in the corridors of power and policy. Countries worldwide are strengthening their legal frameworks against human trafficking, guided by international treaties like the United Nations Protocol to Prevent, Suppress and Punish Trafficking in Persons, especially Women and Children. These laws aim to protect victims, prosecute perpetrators, and prevent the conditions that foster trafficking.

Jewish legal principles offer a unique perspective in shaping these laws. Jewish law, or Halacha, with its deep-rooted emphasis on justice and ethical treatment of individuals, contributes significantly to this legislative process. The Jewish ethos, encapsulated in principles like pikuach nefesh (the preservation of human life) and the prohibition against ona'ah (deception or unfairness), reinforces the moral foundations of anti-trafficking laws. These principles inspire laws that not only penalize traffickers but also focus on protecting and rehabilitating victims, aligning with the Jewish value of preserving dignity and life.

The challenges in implementing and enforcing these laws are considerable, yet the interplay of religious ethics and secular lawmaking provides a robust framework for action. The Jewish voice in this legislative discourse emphasizes the need for laws that reflect not only a commitment to justice but also compassion and empathy for the victims.

In summary, the intersection of interfaith initiatives and legislative efforts forms a dynamic front in the fight against human trafficking. Inspired by Jewish principles and working hand-in-hand with a spectrum of faith communities, this united approach offers a powerful model of action-based, compassionate, and effective strategies to combat this grave human rights issue.

We are reminded that while the path to freedom is fraught with challenges, it is also paved with solidarity, perseverance, and the unyielding pursuit of justice. The narrative leaves us with a call to action, urging each of us to play our part in breaking the chains of modern slavery and lighting the way to freedom.

The narrative pivots to the powerful testimonies of survivors, offering a deeply human perspective on the realities of human trafficking. This chapter provides a platform for survivors to share their experiences, shedding light on the personal struggles and triumphs in their journeys towards liberation and healing.

We begin by introducing the stories of individuals who have endured the horrors of sex trafficking. Their narratives reveal the psychological and physical abuses they faced, as well as the incredible resilience they displayed in overcoming their ordeals. We intersperse these accounts with insights from Jewish authors who have chronicled such stories in non-fiction works, bringing an added depth to the understanding of these experiences.

One such author, Rebecca Bender, a survivor of sex trafficking and now an advocate, shares her story in her book "In Pursuit of Love." Bender's journey from victim to survivor to leader in the anti-trafficking movement exemplifies the transformative power of resilience and hope. Her words resonate with a profound truth: "Survivors don't need our pity; they need our partnership. They need us to stand with them as they rebuild their lives."

Another voice we hear is from Rachel Moran, author of "Paid For: My Journey Through Prostitution." Her raw and honest account of being trafficked in the sex industry in Ireland provides a haunting look into the realities faced by many. Moran's reflections underscore the importance of addressing the root causes of trafficking, including poverty, gender inequality, and societal attitudes towards women and sex.

In profiling the work of Jewish organizations fighting against human trafficking, we bring to light the ethical and religious imperatives that drive their mission. One such organization, T'ruah: The Rabbinic Call for Human Rights, mobilizes rabbis and Jewish communities to advocate for policy changes and support survivors. Their work, grounded in Jewish religious law, reinforces the idea that every human being is created in the image of God and deserves to live a life free from exploitation.

The Vienna Forum

The Vienna Forum - A Convergence of Efforts

In the grand halls of the Vienna Forum, representatives from Member States, United Nations entities, non-governmental and international organizations, the business community, academia, and civil society converge. The atmosphere is charged with a sense of purpose and urgency. The Forum serves as a visible testament to the consolidated support and political will backing the goals of the Global Initiative.

The Forum's objectives are multifaceted: raising awareness of all forms of trafficking, facilitating cooperation and partnerships among participants, assessing progress made, and setting directions for future measures to prevent and counter human trafficking. It provides a platform to evaluate the dimensions of the issue and the actions taken in response, fostering an open environment for practical steps to be taken.

The Vienna Forum is organized around three central themes: Vulnerability, Impact, and Action. Each theme is explored in depth through plenary sessions and workshops, allowing participants to delve into comprehensive anti-trafficking strategies and practical actions.

1. **Vulnerability:** The Forum examines why human trafficking occurs. It addresses issues such as disempowerment, social exclusion, economic vulnerability, natural disasters, conflict, and political turmoil. Discussions focus on decreasing vulnera-

bility as a strategic impact of prevention efforts.

2. **Impact:** Participants explore the human and social consequences of trafficking, sharing experiences and focusing on the traumatic effects on victims, including physical abuse, psychological trauma, adverse health effects, social stigmatization, and the risk of revictimization.

3. **Action:** The Forum reviews global anti-trafficking strategies and national responses. The challenges of implementation, clarity of terms and definitions, national political concerns, and the effectiveness of various measures are discussed to promote systematic, consistent, and sustainable action.

In a poignant moment, Sarah and David, now active participants in the Forum, share their personal stories. Their narratives serve as powerful testaments to the human impact of trafficking and the importance of the Forum's objectives. Sarah, drawing from her Jewish heritage, emphasizes the moral imperative to fight trafficking, resonating with the teachings of the Torah and Talmud on the sanctity of human life.

David, reflecting on his journey from victim to survivor, speaks of the transformative power of collective action and the necessity of a united front against trafficking. His story highlights the critical role of international cooperation and the effectiveness of initiatives like UN.GIFT and the Vienna Forum.

As the Forum progresses, innovative approaches and best practices are shared. The participants discuss the need for comprehensive intervention strategies, ranging from strengthening legal frameworks to empowering vulnerable communities. The importance of public-private partnerships, community engagement, and education in prevention efforts is underscored.

The chapter culminates with a call to action, echoing the words of Elie Wiesel, emphasizing the duty to take sides against oppression and injustice. The Vienna Forum serves as a beacon of hope and a catalyst for change, galvanizing participants and observers alike to take concrete steps in their spheres of influence to combat human trafficking.

As the narrative closes this chapter, it leaves an indelible impression of the collective strength and resolve of the global community in the face of this grave challenge. The Vienna Forum stands as a testament to the power of collaboration and the unyielding spirit of those dedicated to eradicating human trafficking and upholding the values of justice, compassion, and human dignity. This story of struggle and triumph continues to inspire and propel forward the ongoing fight against one of the most pressing human rights issues of our time.Through this narrative readers gain not only a deeper understanding of the harrowing realities of human trafficking but also the indomitable strength of those who have lived through it. Their stories serve as a rallying cry for continued action and a reminder of the enduring human spirit.

CHAIN BREAKING PROTOCOL

In "Breaking The Chains of Modern Slavery," we entered the intricate realm of human trafficking, where diverse organizations, including law enforcement, non-profits, and grassroots movements, engage in a tireless crusade for justice and victim protection. As we continue the saga unfolds with an examination of law enforcement's pivotal role in combatting trafficking. Their challenges are immense: identifying victims concealed in plain sight and building substantial cases against shadowy traffickers. Highlighted within this narrative are successful sting operations and rescue missions, showcasing the profound impact of coordinated law enforcement efforts.

Parallel to these efforts are the endeavors of non-profit organizations, offering an array of essential services to survivors, from shelter and medical aid to legal and psychological support. Their holistic approach is vital in aiding individuals to reconstruct their lives post-trafficking.

Additionally, the narrative shines a spotlight on grassroots movements. Their novel strategies in raising awareness and advocating for change harness the power of community engagement and social media, spotlighting trafficking and spurring action.

Interwoven with this is the transnational law of trafficking as outlined in the United Nations Convention against Transnational Organized Crime and the accompanying Palermo Protocol. These instruments, established to promote cooperation among States, aim to effectively prevent and combat trafficking. The Protocol is not confined to cross-border trafficking but includes internal trafficking within a State, involving organized criminal groups operating in multiple States.

The Protocol's definition of 'Trafficking in Persons' encompasses various forms of coercion for exploitation, ranging from sexual exploitation and forced labor to servitude and organ removal. This international framework, however, faces the challenge of diverse domestic interpretations and applications by States party to the Protocol.

The narrative also delves into the Rome Statute of the International Criminal Court, which, while not criminalizing trafficking per se, addresses it within the context of the crime against humanity of enslavement. This inclusion brings the issue into the realm of international judicial consideration.

Thus, as the story unfolds, it becomes evident that the fight against human trafficking is a complex mosaic of local and global efforts. Law enforcement agencies, non-profit organizations, and grassroots movements work in tandem with international legal frameworks, each playing a crucial role in addressing this multifaceted issue. The narrative highlights the need for a coordinated response that spans from local communities to the global stage, reflecting the multifaceted nature of human trafficking and the necessity for a united front in combating this transnational crime.

As the narrative progresses, it becomes evident that the battle against human trafficking requires more than just a coordinated response; it demands a deep understanding of the root causes and a commitment to addressing them. This is where the role of education and advocacy becomes paramount. Educational initiatives aimed at raising awareness about the signs of trafficking and preventive measures are crucial in stopping this crime at its source. Advocacy efforts, meanwhile, focus on influencing policy and legislation, ensuring that laws are not only well-crafted but also effectively implemented and enforced.

The story then shifts to the personal experiences of those who have been directly affected by human trafficking. These are not just stories of suffering and exploitation but also of resilience and hope. The narratives of survivors provide invaluable insights into the mechanics of trafficking networks and the methods used to lure and trap victims. Their stories also highlight the long road to recovery that survivors must travel, underscoring the importance of comprehensive support systems, including legal aid, psychological counseling, and job training.

The interplay between local actions and global policies is also a critical aspect of this narrative. While international protocols and conventions set the framework for combatting human trafficking, it is the on-the-ground efforts of local organizations and communities that make a tangible difference. These grassroots efforts, often led by survivors themselves, are crucial in providing immediate assistance to victims, raising awareness within communities, and advocating for policy changes at the local and national levels.

As the chapter draws to a close, the focus shifts to the future. The narrative emphasizes the need for continuous vigilance and adaptation in strategies to combat human trafficking. With the ever-evolving tactics of traffickers, the responses too must evolve. This includes leveraging technology to track and combat trafficking networks, as well as developing more effective ways to support and reintegrate survivors into society.

In conclusion, the narrative of "Breaking The Chains of Modern Slavery" paints a comprehensive picture of the fight against human trafficking. It's a story that intertwines the efforts of law enforcement, non-profits, grassroots movements, and international legal frameworks. It's a tale of resilience in the face of adversity, of communities coming together to combat a global scourge, and of a continuous journey towards justice and human dignity. As the saga continues, it leaves the readers with a sense of urgency and a call to action, reminding them that the fight against human trafficking is far from over and that everyone has a role to play in this global endeavor.As the narrative advances, it becomes increasingly clear that the battle against human trafficking requires not only a patchwork of localized initiatives but also a cohesive, global strategy. The synergy between grassroots activism, non-profit support systems, law enforcement operations, and international legal frameworks forms the backbone of this global effort.

The narrative then shifts focus to the unique challenges and innovations at the grassroots level. These movements, often spearheaded by survivors and local activists, bring a crucial, on-the-ground perspective to the fight against trafficking. They employ creative tactics, from community education programs to social media campaigns, that not only raise awareness but also empower local communities to take action. Their efforts underscore the importance of local knowledge and community engagement in both preventing trafficking and aiding survivors in their recovery journey.

In tandem with grassroots initiatives, the role of non-profits is further examined. These organizations bridge the gap between law enforcement's pursuit of justice and the survivors' need for comprehensive care. They offer safe havens, legal assistance, and psychological support, tailoring their services to address the complex needs of trafficking survivors. Their work is vital in ensuring that once rescued, survivors have the resources and support they need to heal and rebuild their lives.

Meanwhile, law enforcement agencies continue to face the arduous task of dismantling trafficking networks. Their operations, often in collaboration with international bodies, highlight the necessity for cross-border cooperation and intelligence sharing. These agencies not only work on rescuing victims but also on gathering evidence to bring traffickers to justice. Their efforts are often hampered by the covert and transnational nature of trafficking rings, requiring sophisticated tactics and technologies to track and apprehend perpetrators.

At the international level, the enforcement of the Palermo Protocol and related statutes underscores the complexity of legislating against a crime as multifaceted and borderless as human trafficking. The narrative emphasizes the need for countries to harmonize their legal definitions and approaches to effectively combat trafficking. This harmonization is crucial in ensuring that traffickers cannot exploit legal loopholes or discrepancies between national laws.

The narrative concludes by reiterating the need for a multi-pronged approach to effectively combat human trafficking. It calls for continued collaboration across all sectors - law enforcement, non-profits, grassroots movements, and international bodies - to create a united front against this global scourge. By combining the strengths and expertise of each sector, the fight against human trafficking can be more strategic, more effective, and ultimately more successful in protecting the vulnerable and bringing perpetrators to justice. This united effort not only symbolizes a commitment to eradicating human trafficking but also reflects a collective dedication to upholding human dignity and rights across the globe.

We also discuss the role of faith-based organizations in the fight against trafficking. These organizations draw on religious teachings to inspire and guide their work, emphasizing the moral imperative to combat this form of modern slavery. Examples include the work of The Coalition of Catholic Organizations Against Human Trafficking (CCOAHT),the Jewish Coalition Against

Trafficking and the National Council of Jewish Women, which have made significant contributions to anti-trafficking efforts.

A significant focus is on the role of Jewish religious law as a moral compass guiding these efforts. We delve into the teachings and interpretations of Jewish texts that unequivocally condemn slavery and human trafficking as moral abominations. This perspective is juxtaposed against the viewpoint that justifies slavery for economic gain, showcasing the ethical superiority of the Jewish stance.

One prominent voice in this battle is that of Rabbi Dr. Shmuly Yanklowitz, an influential Jewish ethicist and activist. In his writings, Yanklowitz argues passionately against the commodification of human beings, emphasizing the Jewish principle of every person being created in the image of God. "Jewish law, with its profound emphasis on human dignity and freedom, inherently rejects any form of slavery or human exploitation," he asserts.

In addition to religious leaders, the chapter features quotes from survivors of human trafficking. Their firsthand accounts provide a poignant and powerful testimony to the horrors they endured and the strength they found to overcome them. These stories are not just narratives of survival but also powerful tools for advocacy and change.

The chapter also highlights the work of international organizations, such as the United Nations, in their efforts to combat trafficking. We examine how these organizations use their global platforms to advocate for stronger laws, provide support to affected countries, and foster international cooperation against this transnational crime.

Amidst these narratives, we encounter a powerful quote from Elie Wiesel, Nobel Laureate and Holocaust survivor, who once said, "We must always take sides. Neutrality helps the oppressor, never the victim. Silence encourages the tormentor, never the tormented." This call to action res-onates throughout the chapter, urging readers to engage actively in the fight against trafficking.

As we move on with the saga the narrative serves as both a summation of the journey so far and a blueprint for future action against human trafficking. This chapter synthesizes the insights gathered from previous chapters and outlines a strategic approach to intensify the fight against this heinous crime.

In the battle against human trafficking, the adoption of the Protocol to Prevent, Suppress, and Punish Trafficking in Persons marked a turning point, ushering in a new era of legislative frameworks and international cooperation. This story is not just about laws and policies; it's about the lives they impact, the societies they shape, and the moral compass they provide in a world often blurred by ethical ambiguities.

The narrative opens with a reflection on the current state of human trafficking and the progress made to date. It acknowledges the challenges that remain, emphasizing the need for sustained and intensified efforts. The narrative then shifts to presenting a comprehensive strategy that encompasses prevention, protection, prosecution, and partnership.

Prevention strategies are discussed in detail, focusing on education, awareness-raising, and addressing the root causes of trafficking such as poverty, inequality, and lack of opportunities. The narrative stresses the importance of community involvement and the role of faith-based organizations, like those in the Jewish community, in prevention efforts.

The protection of victims and survivors is highlighted as a critical component of the strategy. The chapter explores the need for comprehensive support services, including legal aid, psychological counseling, and reintegration programs. It also emphasizes the importance of survivor-led initiatives, which bring invaluable perspectives and credibility to the fight against trafficking.

As nations around the world began to align with the Protocol, new laws emerged, each seeking to define and penalize the scourge of human trafficking. However, the road was riddled with challenges: inconsistencies in definitions and gaps in implementation. The Torah's teaching, "Justice, justice you shall pursue" (Deuteronomy 16:20), echoed as a guiding principle, reminding us that the pursuit of justice is a continuous and evolving journey. This chapter delves into the complexities of shaping laws that not only punish traffickers but also protect the victims.

Prosecution of traffickers stands as a crucial deterrent. Yet, the path to justice is fraught with hurdles – from the need for victim cooperation to the complexity of transnational crimes. The Talmud's wisdom, "Whoever saves a single life, it is as if they have saved an entire world" (Sanhedrin 37a), inspires a relentless pursuit of justice for each victim. This chapter explores the intricacies of legal battles, the need for enhanced law enforcement training, and the vital role of international cooperation.

Collaboration emerges as a formidable weapon in this fight. Governments, NGOs, faith-based organizations, the private sector, and international bodies come together, each bringing unique strengths to the table. The story of the Jewish Coalition Against Trafficking and the National Council of Jewish Women exemplifies how faith-driven initiatives can galvanize communities and foster change. This chapter celebrates successful multi-stakeholder partnerships, showcasing how united efforts amplify the impact against trafficking.

As this comprehensive treatise on human trafficking approaches its final chapters, it underscores the necessity for an ongoing, comprehensive strategy to obliterate this global scourge. It extends an invitation to readers worldwide, urging them to become part of this international crusade. Leviticus 19:16 serves as a moral beacon, inspiring a call to proactive involvement rather than passive observation in this crucial battle.

Central to this narrative is the profound influence of Jewish religious law, serving as a cornerstone of moral and ethical direction. The text revisits these age-old teachings, showcasing their role in guiding those who stand against the tide of human trafficking. This ethical guidepost, deeply rooted in the quest for justice and human dignity, presents a stark contrast to perspectives that seek to justify or diminish the severity of human trafficking's brutalities.

In the heart of a relentless war against human trafficking, a tapestry of heroes emerges – law enforcement agencies, non-profit organizations, grassroots movements, and international collaborations. Each entity plays a pivotal role in this global fight, an intricate ballet of justice, rescue, and rehabilitation.

The story begins with law enforcement agencies, the frontline warriors in this battle. Tasked with the monumental challenge of unearthing hidden victims and dismantling the clandestine networks of traffickers, these agencies represent hope and justice. A prime example is the Federal Bureau of Investigation (FBI) with its dedicated Human Trafficking Program. Their mission – to identify, disrupt, and dismantle trafficking rings – is a testament to their commitment. The FBI's operations, marked by successful sting operations and high-stakes rescue missions, demonstrate the power of persistent and coordinated law enforcement efforts.

Another notable agency is Interpol, the international police organization. With its global reach and collaborative approach, Interpol plays a crucial role in combating human trafficking across borders. Their joint operations with national law enforcement agencies have led to the arrest of numerous traffickers and the rescue of victims worldwide. Additionally, organizations like Homeland Security Investigations (HSI) and the United Nations Office on Drugs and Crime (UNODC) actively work to combat human trafficking through intelligence gathering, investigations, and international cooperation. These agencies, along with many others, are at the forefront of the fight against human trafficking, tirelessly working to bring traffickers to justice and provide support to survivors.

Yet, the journey of a trafficking survivor does not end with rescue. Here, non-profit organizations step in, providing the much-needed sanctuary and support. Among them is the Polaris Project, operating the National Human Trafficking Hotline, a beacon of hope for victims seeking a way out. Their mission is not just to assist survivors but to prevent trafficking and raise awareness about this hidden crime. Polaris, with its ethos of eradication and empowerment, embodies the dedication required in this fight.

An essential thread in this narrative is the role of grassroots movements. These community-driven forces are the undercurrent of change, raising awareness, and advocating for policy reforms. One such organization is the Coalition Against Trafficking in Women (CATW), which tirelessly works to prevent trafficking and promote gender equality. Their mission statement resounds with a commitment to challenging the root causes of trafficking and championing systemic change.

In this coalition of hope, Jewish representatives play a significant role, bringing their rich heritage of social justice and tikkun olam – healing the world. The Jewish Coalition Against Trafficking (JCAT) stands out, mobilizing the Jewish community against modern-day slavery. Their mission, rooted in the values of justice, compassion, and solidarity, amplifies the call to action against trafficking.

As we delve deeper into this narrative, we find factual examples that highlight the success of interfaith initiatives led by Jewish leaders in government and religion. One such initiative is Safe Haven, a non-profit organization that offers a comprehensive suite of services – including shelter, medical care, and legal assistance – to trafficking survivors. In an interview, Rabbi Cohen, the founder of Hope Renewed, shared, 'Survivors often face immense trauma. Our specialized counseling services, led by Jewish leaders, are crucial in helping them overcome their past and build a brighter future.' These words echo the profound impact of these interfaith organizations in aiding survivors on their road to recovery.

Globally, the fight against trafficking is bolstered by international treaties and collaborative efforts. The United Nations Convention against Transnational Organized Crime and the Palermo Protocol set the stage for a unified global response. This international legal framework, coupled with national efforts, forms the backbone of the global strategy against trafficking.

As the volume draws to a close, it imparts a message of hope and resilience. It highlights the progress made and optimistically looks forward to future victories. This narrative empowers readers, inviting them to join the journey towards a world free from the clutches of trafficking. It showcases the diverse approaches and collective impact of these efforts, inspiring support and participation in this crucial cause.

The concluding call to action is compelling, encouraging readers to join the global effort against human trafficking. It converts insights into actionable steps, providing guidance to individuals and communities on how to create a significant impact. From identifying signs of trafficking to participating in policy advocacy, the text offers a roadmap for getting involved.

This narrative takes readers on a journey into the heart of a global crisis - human trafficking.

It showcases the power of unity, resilience, and moral courage in tackling one of the most pressing human rights challenges of our time. By shedding light on this issue, it aims to inspire and empower readers to join the global crusade against human trafficking.

MUSLIM-BACKED INITIATIVES AGAINST SLAVERY: UNITING FAITH AND ACTION PART ONE

The Islamic Society of North America (ISNA) is the first Islamic religious organization in the world to elect a Muslim woman to the position of president. This was done through authentic scriptural understanding and interpretation, and has led to other local and regional mosques and organizations opening doors to women in leadership positions.

There are Muslim women scholars of Islamic Shariah and jurisprudence on Dr. Ingrid Mattson – the Board of the Islamic Fiqh Council of North America, a body that issues fatwas (religious legal opinions on important issues). These new roles for women in the American community have empowered American Muslims to express opposition to traditions within the Muslim world that have resulted in a narrow interpretation of the Quran and the traditions of our Prophet and in some cases may have been falsely considered to be integral to Islamic tradition.

For example, some Muslim immigrants coming from countries like the Sudan, Egypt, and Somalia thought that the prevailing custom of genital mutilation in their countries had its roots in Islam and therefore saw it as an Islamic religious obligation to continue this practice in the U.S. ISNA was clear from the beginning that genital mutilation may have been a practice in some African countries, but there is no basis for it in the Quran or in the traditions of the Prophet. The Muslim community in North America has also taken a position against child marriage and forced marriage.

Our Fiqh Council scholars took a position against polygamy and reinforced commitment to monogamy by arguing that the prevailing law must be followed and that polygamy made it impossible to treat all wives equally as the Quran requires. The Prophet Muhammad declared clearly that Almighty Allah will not accept the prayers and fasting from a believer who enslaves free human beings. The enslavement or exploitation of the helpless is considered a sin of the highest order, in fact, a rebellion against the divine law.

The Muslim community in the United States and around the world has also been involved directly and indirectly in fighting against human trafficking. They are involved in various efforts, including providing role models and enhancing awareness and education about the evils of human trafficking. Many Muslim activists, men and women, are involved in advocacy and charity through various interfaith and Islamic organizations.

The United Nations Office on Drugs and Crime published a document, "Combating Trafficking in Persons in Accordance with the Principles of Islamic Law" which serves as a point of reference for many Muslim organizations. According to this document, "the Islamic prohibition of trafficking in persons is therefore based on a comprehensive set of principles is solidly grounded in the Islamic legal tradition that, taken together, not only criminalize the act of trafficking in persons but also prevent such an act, and protect victims of that crime." And further, "the rules of international law and the principles of Islamic law are clearly complementary to each other in effectively and comprehensively combating trafficking in persons."In the labyrinth of our contemporary world, where shadows of an age-old evil still lurk, a compelling saga emerges. This narrative, rich in intrigue and suspense, reveals the persistent reality of modern slavery – a scourge that challenges the essence of human dignity. At the heart of this tale is a document of profound significance, "Combating Trafficking in Persons in Accordance with the Principles of Islamic Law," published by the United Nations Office on Drugs and Crime. This pivotal work serves as a beacon of guidance for numerous Muslim organizations, casting light on a path shrouded in darkness.

The story begins in a world grappling with the hidden yet pervasive chains of forced labor, human trafficking, and debt bondage. Within this realm, the document stands as a testament to the enduring principles of Islamic Law, opposing these forms of modern-day slavery. It declares with unwavering clarity that the Islamic prohibition of trafficking in persons is grounded in a comprehensive set of principles, deeply rooted in the Islamic legal tradition. This tradition not only criminalizes the act of trafficking but also lays the foundation for preventing such heinous acts and protecting its victims.

As the narrative unfolds, we are introduced to a diverse array of characters, each playing a crucial role in this metaphysical battle against human exploitation. There are scholars and activists, each drawing inspiration from the document to challenge the status quo. They interpret its teachings to confront modern slavery, weaving a tapestry of resistance against exploitation and advocating for the voiceless.

In a poignant scene, we witness a powerful moment of realization among the characters. They recognize that their struggle is not only against the overt acts of inhumanity but also against the systemic failings that allow such atrocities to thrive. Current immigration policies and societal indifference often serve as unwitting accomplices to these crimes against humanity, leaving the most vulnerable exposed to the predations of modern-day slavers.

As the story progresses, the characters embark on a journey of transformation. They engage in a collective quest to reshape perceptions and implement change, driven by the teachings of the document. They advocate for policies that uphold human rights and dignity, supporting organizations tirelessly working to bring light to the dark corners of exploitation.

The climax of this saga is a moment of profound unity and determination. The characters, having traversed a path fraught with challenges, find strength in their shared vision. They form an alliance, transcending religious, cultural, and national boundaries, united in their resolve to eradicate the malignant growth of slavery that festers in society's shadows.

In the concluding scenes, we witness a renewed sense of purpose among the characters. They leave with a commitment to confront the darkness with the light of their faith, their actions fueled by the teachings of the document and the principles of Islamic Law. This is not just a chapter in a book; it's a living testament to the enduring struggle for freedom and dignity.

This saga, interwoven with elements of suspense, intrigue, and metaphysical depth, ends with a clarion call to action. It serves as a reminder that the fight for freedom is far from over, and it's a battle that must be waged with the combined might of faith, love, and unwavering conviction. The story of "Combating Trafficking in Persons in Accordance with the Principles of Islamic Law" thus becomes a narrative of hope, resilience, and the relentless pursuit of a world where every individual is valued, every voice is heard, and every life is free from the grasp of tyranny.

In the labyrinth of our contemporary world, where shadows of an age-old evil still lurk, a compelling saga emerges. This narrative, rich in intrigue and suspense, reveals the persistent reality of modern slavery – a scourge that challenges the essence of human dignity. At the heart of this tale is a document of profound significance, "Combating Trafficking in Persons in Accordance with the Principles of Islamic Law," published by the United Nations Office on Drugs and Crime. This pivotal work serves as a beacon of guidance for numerous Muslim organizations, casting light on a path shrouded in darkness.

The story begins in a world grappling with the hidden yet pervasive chains of forced labor, human trafficking, and debt bondage. Within this realm, the document stands as a testament to the enduring principles of Islamic Law, opposing these forms of modern-day slavery. It declares with unwavering clarity that the Islamic prohibition of trafficking in persons is grounded in a comprehensive set of principles, deeply rooted in the Islamic legal tradition. This tradition not only criminalizes the act of trafficking but also lays the foundation for preventing such heinous acts and protecting its victims.

As the narrative unfolds, we are introduced to a diverse array of characters, each playing a crucial role in this metaphysical battle against human exploitation. There are scholars and activists, each drawing inspiration from the document to challenge the status quo. They interpret its teachings to confront modern slavery, weaving a tapestry of resistance against exploitation and advocating for the voiceless.

In a poignant scene, we witness a powerful moment of realization among the characters. They recognize that their struggle is not only against the overt acts of inhumanity but also against the systemic failings that allow such atrocities to thrive. Current immigration policies and societal indifference often serve as unwitting accomplices to these crimes against humanity, leaving the most vulnerable exposed to the predations of modern-day slavers.

As the story progresses, the characters embark on a journey of transformation. They engage in a collective quest to reshape perceptions and implement change, driven by the teachings of the document. They advocate for policies that uphold human rights and dignity, supporting organizations tirelessly working to bring light to the dark corners of exploitation.

The climax of this saga is a moment of profound unity and determination. The characters, having traversed a path fraught with challenges, find strength in their shared vision. They form an alliance, transcending religious, cultural, and national boundaries, united in their resolve to eradicate the malignant growth of slavery that festers in society's shadows.

In the concluding scenes, we witness a renewed sense of purpose among the characters. They leave with a commitment to confront the darkness with the light of their faith, their actions fueled by the teachings of the document and the principles of

Islamic Law. This is not just a chapter in a book; it's a living testament to the enduring struggle for freedom and dignity.

This saga, interwoven with elements of suspense, intrigue, and metaphysical depth, ends with a clarion call to action. It serves as a reminder that the fight for freedom is far from over, and it's a battle that must be waged with the combined might of faith, love, and unwavering conviction. The story of "Combating Trafficking in Persons in Accordance with the Principles of Islamic Law" thus becomes a narrative of hope, resilience, and the relentless pursuit of a world where every individual is valued, every voice is heard, and every life is free from the grasp of tyranny.

Muslim-Backed Initiatives Against Slavery: Uniting Faith and Action Part Two

In the captivating realm of our world's narrative, where the complexities of morality can sometimes cloud our understanding, there exists a compelling and enlightening story that demands to be shared. It is a tale deeply rooted in profound philosophical reflections, where moral reasoning, suspense, and exploration intertwine to weave a narrative that resonates on a profound level. This captivating saga, drawing inspiration from modern literary masterpieces on the Islamic revulsion of slavery, sheds light on the intricate web of human trafficking, a persistent menace that plagues humanity in diverse manifestations.

"At the heart of this narrative lies a document of significant importance - 'Combating Trafficking in Persons in Accordance with the Principles of Islamic Law,' published by the United Nations Office on Drugs and Crime. This pivotal document serves as a cornerstone for numerous Muslim-backed initiatives worldwide, providing a framework that combines the profound wisdom of Islamic law with the urgent mission to combat human trafficking."

Title: Muslim-Backed Initiatives Against Slavery: Uniting Faith and Action

Introduction:

In the fight against slavery and human trafficking, Muslim organizations around the world have been at the forefront, driven by a shared commitment to justice and compassion. At the heart of this global movement lies a document of significant importance - 'Combating Trafficking in Persons in Accordance with the Principles of Islamic Law,' published by the United Nations Office on Drugs and Crime. This pivotal document serves as a cornerstone for numerous Muslim-backed initiatives, providing a framework that combines the profound wisdom of Islamic law with the urgent mission to combat human trafficking.

1. The United Nations Office on Drugs and Crime:

   The United Nations Office on Drugs and Crime (UNODC) has played a crucial role in addressing human trafficking. Their document, 'Combating Trafficking in Persons in Accordance with the Principles of Islamic Law,' has been instrumental in guiding Muslim organizations in their efforts to combat this heinous crime. By aligning the principles of Islamic law with international standards, the UNODC has fostered a global movement against human trafficking.

2. Islamic Relief Worldwide:
Islamic Relief Worldwide, a prominent Muslim humanitarian organization, has been actively involved in combating slavery and human trafficking. They have implemented various initiatives aimed at raising awareness, providing support to survivors, and advocating for stronger legislation against trafficking. Their work exemplifies the commitment of Muslim organizations to address this grave issue.

3. Muslim Women's Organizations:
Muslim women's organizations have also played a vital role in the fight against slavery. These organizations have been instrumental in empowering women and

girls who are vulnerable to trafficking. Through education, vocational training, and economic empowerment programs, they provide opportunities for individuals to break free from the cycle of exploitation.

4. Faith-Based Coalitions:
Faith-based coalitions have emerged as powerful forces in the fight against slavery. These coalitions bring together Muslim organizations, interfaith groups, and civil society organizations to collectively combat human trafficking. By leveraging their shared values and resources, they amplify their impact and create lasting change.

Conclusion:
Muslim-backed initiatives against slavery and human trafficking are rooted in the principles of jus-

tice, compassion, and the profound wisdom of Islamic law. The document published by the United Nations Office on Drugs and Crime serves as a guiding light, providing a framework for Muslim organizations to combat this grave violation of human rights. Through their collective efforts, these initiatives are making a significant impact in the fight against slavery, offering hope and support to survivors, and working towards a world free from the chains of exploitation.

The essence of the document lies in its proclamation that the prohibition of trafficking in persons is deeply embedded in Islamic law, grounded in a comprehensive set of principles. These principles are not mere abstract notions but are firmly rooted in the Islamic legal tradition, offering a potent blend of spiritual guidance and practical action to address this global crisis.

As our story unfolds, we witness the embodiment of these principles in the actions of various Muslim organizations. They draw inspiration from the document, using its teachings to fuel their efforts against the dark trade of human lives. Through their endeavors, these organizations illuminate the paths of those ensnared in the shadows of trafficking, offering hope and a way towards freedom.

The narrative weaves together examples and quotes from the document, each one a thread in the larger fabric of the fight against trafficking. These words serve as beacons of light, guiding the efforts of those committed to eradicating this form of modern-day slavery. They remind us that in the fight against human trafficking, every action, grounded in faith and justice, can make a profound difference.

The story takes us on a journey through different landscapes of human experience – from bustling city streets where the vulnerable are preyed upon, to quiet community gatherings where strategies are forged and alliances are built. In these settings, the principles of the UN document come to life, shaping the actions and motivations of those who stand against the tide of trafficking.

Each character in our saga, driven by a unique blend of faith and determination, contributes to the unfolding drama. Their actions, informed by the teachings of the document and their own moral compass, create ripples that extend far beyond their immediate surroundings.

As the story approaches its climax, we are reminded that the fight against human trafficking is a continuous battle, one that demands resilience, collaboration, and a deep understanding of the ethical and moral dimensions of our actions. The principles outlined in the UN document are not just rules to be followed but are calls to action, urging us to rise above indifference and to engage actively in the quest for justice and human dignity.

In the end, our narrative is more than just a collection of events; it is a testament to the power of faith, law, and collective action in confronting one of the gravest challenges of our time. It is a story that calls upon each of us to reflect on our role in this fight and to step forward with courage and conviction, armed with the wisdom of the past and the hope for a better future.

This is a saga not just of struggle but of hope – a hope that shines brightly against the backdrop of a world often marred by darkness. It is a story that resonates on a metaphysical level, urging us to look beyond the surface and to grasp the deeper truths that guide our journey towards a world free of trafficking and exploitation.

HOW DO I GET INVOLVED

"We could eradicate slavery. The laws are in place. The multi-nationals, the world trade organizations, the United Nations, they could end slavery, but they're not going to do it until and unless we demand it." — Kevin Bales, Free the Slaves

Take Action: How Do I Get Involved as an Individual, Group or UNICEF Club Member? Now that you've learned about the issue and what organizations around the world are doing to combat human trafficking, you may be wondering what you can do to help. The good news is that there's a lot you can do! Following are 21 ways to get involved.

1. Join or start a UNICEF Club at your high school or college. Dedicate a week to raising awareness about human trafficking. Visit: unicefusa.org/highschool or unicefusa.org/campusinitiative to get involved.

2. Post the National Human Trafficking Hotline , around your neighborhood, school, or workplace. The hotline handles calls from anyone, including witnesses, potential victims, service providers, community members, and people hoping to learn more. It is toll-free and can be reached anywhere in the U.S., 24 hours a day, 365 days a year. You can download a flyer for free at polarisproject.org/resources/outreach-and-awareness-materials, or download our Hotline Postcard from our Resources page at unicefusa.org/endtr

afficking. Please ask permission before posting flyers in coffee shops, restaurants, business locations, etc.

3. Teach your students about human trafficking. Check out our K-12 educator resources for lesson plans and activities for your students at teachunicef.org.

4. Find out how the work of exploited people has a direct effect on your life. Visit the Slavery Footprint website to take an online survey that helps you determine how many slaves touch the products you buy. Through the site's action center and mobile app, consumers are invited to take action and call for ethically sourced products. Visit: slaveryfootprint.org.

5. Learn how to spot the signs of human trafficking by visiting: polarisproject.org /signs.

6. A child's vulnerability to trafficking can be greatly reduced by the consistent presence of a caring adult. Invest in the life of a young girl or boy in your community by volunteering as a tutor or mentor. Get connected to an organization near you at mentoring.org.

7. Host a panel discussion. Speakers could include local experts in the field, a professor knowledgeable on the subject of human trafficking, a member of law enforcement, or a survivor of trafficking.

8. Keep learning. Sign up for Google alerts about human trafficking or a newsletter from an anti-trafficking organization like the Polaris Project or International Justice Mission.

9. Write an article about human trafficking for your local or school newspaper or

community blog. Don't feel comfortable writing it yourself? Write to the editors of the paper and ask them to do a piece on it.

10. Change the conversation by working within your social circles. A "pimp" is not a cool guy, but someone who abuses and exploits women. A "prostitute" is often a victim of sexual exploitation. Help your friends rethink their choice of language. For tips on how to talk about these issues, visit: againstourwill.org/how-to-talk-about-it.

11. Volunteer your skills. Do pro bono legal work, promote products made by survivors, or create an artistic piece to raise awareness about human trafficking.

12. A Call to Men: Men have an important role to play in ending human trafficking. "A Call to Men" shares ways for men to

speak out against domestic violence, rape, and human trafficking, visit acalltomen.org. Also, check out Man Up at manupcampaign.org.

13. Walk for freedom. Join or organize a walk in your city to raise awareness about human trafficking.

14. Organize a fundraiser to benefit UNICEF's work to protect children. For tips and ideas on how to fundraise, sign up as a UNICEF volunteer at unicefusa.org/actioncenter and fill out an event application form at unicefusa.org/fundraiser.

15. Host a screening of Not My Life or another film focused on the issue of human trafficking. Facilitate a discussion afterward about ways to take action. Email endtrafficking@unicefusa.org to learn how

you can get a copy of Not My Life along with a discussion guide.

16. Petition the President of the United States. Ask the President to sign the Convention on the Rights of the Child. This international treaty recognizes that children are not possessions, but people who have human rights. Visit: unicefusa.org/advocate to learn more.

17. Switch to Fair Trade brands, and/or host a Fair Trade Party. Fair Trade certified products are produced without slave or child labor. Profits from Fair Trade products support farmers and laborers involved in production and ensure that they are paid fairly and work under safe conditions. To learn more, visit: fairtradeusa.org. Download our Fair Trade Event Kit from our Resources page at unicefusa.org/endtraff

icking.

18. Dedicate a sporting event to raising awareness about human trafficking. Get the team involved, have proceeds from the game go to a local anti-trafficking organization. Feature an info session at halftime and show a short video clip, have a guest speaker, or read a survivor's story. For video suggestions visit mtvU's Against Our Will campaign againstourwill.org/v ideos.

19. Purchase products made by survivors of human trafficking. From jewelry and handbags to lotion and soccer balls — purchasing survivor-made products helps to support sustainable employment and rehabilitation programs for survivors. Start shopping. Visit: polarisproject.org/take-action/raise-awar

eness/buy-products-made-by-survivors.

20. Be a child-safe tourist. Children in tourist areas are especially vulnerable to physical, emotional, and sexual abuse. Learn how to take simple actions to minimize harm to children at childsafetourism.org.

21. Advocate for state laws addressing human trafficking. Visit: polarisproject.org/what-we-do/policy-advocacy/state-policy. Advocate for victims by visiting change.org.

Referance and FAQs

The history of the abolitionist movement and its key figures provides a powerful context for understanding the current challenges in the fight against modern slavery. This in-depth exploration aims to be compelling, informative, and humanitarian, drawing parallels between the past and present struggles against enslavement.

Historical Foundations of Abolition

William Wilberforce, a name synonymous with the abolitionist movement, was born on August 24, 1759, in Hull, England. He grew up in a prosperous merchant family, which allowed him to receive a privileged education at St. John's College, Cambridge. It was during his time at Cambridge that Wilberforce began to cultivate the speaking skills that would later make him an influential orator.

In 1780, at just 21 years of age, Wilberforce embarked on his political career, becoming a Member of Parliament for Kingston upon Hull. Initially, he was more interested in socializing and enjoying the privileges of his position. However, a significant transformation occurred in his life in the early 1780s. A profound religious experience led him to embrace evangelical Christianity, deeply influencing his future path and commitments.

Wilberforce's spiritual awakening brought a new purpose to his life. He became increasingly concerned with social reform and was particularly horrified by the brutality of the transatlantic slave trade. His Christian faith instilled in him a sense of moral obligation to challenge this inhuman practice. His position in Parliament provided him a platform to voice his concerns and initiate change.

In 1787, Wilberforce was approached by Thomas Clarkson and a group of anti-slavery activists. They presented him with detailed evidence of the atrocities of the slave trade, which galvanized Wilberforce's resolve to campaign against it. The same year marked the beginning of his tireless efforts to abolish the slave trade. He became the leading voice in Parliament advocating for its termination.

Wilberforce's struggle was not an easy one. He faced strong opposition from those who benefited economically from the slave trade. Despite the setbacks, including numerous defeats of his motions in Parliament, he remained steadfast in his cause. His eloquence, moral conviction, and unwavering commitment kept the issue at the forefront of public and political debate.

In 1807, after years of relentless campaigning, Wilberforce's efforts finally bore fruit. The Slave Trade Act was passed, making the trading of slaves illegal within the British Empire. While this was a significant victory, Wilberforce knew that the fight was not over. Slavery itself was still legal, and he continued to campaign for its complete abolition.

Wilberforce's health began to decline in the late 1820s, but he remained committed to the abolitionist cause until the end. In 1833, just days before his death on July 29, he received the news that the Slavery Abolition Act had been passed, ensuring the freedom of slaves in most of the British Empire. This news brought a peaceful conclusion to his lifelong struggle against slavery.

William Wilberforce's legacy is monumental. He is remembered not only for his role in ending the slave trade and slavery in the British Empire but also as a pioneer in the promotion of human rights. His life is a testament to the power of perseverance, moral conviction, and the ability to effect significant change through peaceful means. Wilberforce's journey from a life of privilege to one of profound social impact continues to inspire generations in the fight for justice and equality.

Other Great Anti-Salvery Activist:

- **Sojourner Truth:** Born into enslavement in 1797, Truth emerged as a formidable advocate for human rights and women's suffrage. Her iconic speech, "Ain't I a Woman?", remains a poignant reminder of the intersection between racial and gender-based oppression.

- **Harriet Tubman:** Despite suffering from seizures and narcolepsy, Tubman was a pivotal figure in the Underground Railroad, risking her life to lead many to freedom.

- **Frederick Douglass:** His transformation from a slave to a key leader in the abolitionist movement was catalyzed by his powerful memoir, shedding light on the horrors of slavery.

- **William Lloyd Garrison:** Founder of "The Liberator", Garrison's journalistic endeavors significantly contributed to the widespread call for immediate emancipation.

These individuals used various mediums, including speeches and writings, to challenge the in-

stitution of slavery and advocate for racial equality.

(About this referance material, it was used extensively for reference facts for the manuscripot titled "Breaking Chains". It saved much time and research but the premise of the battle against human Trafficking is eloquently stated and rather than deprive the reader of the referances I have chosen to include this efffort out of respect for the need for all opponents of human trafficking might have this referance to enable them to expand beyond the scope of this book.)

Exploitation Creep and the Unmaking of Human Trafficking Law"

In the thought-provoking article "Exploitation Creep and the Unmaking of Human Trafficking Law" from the American Journal of International Law, the author delves into the dynamic and often misunderstood realm of human trafficking legislation. This insightful piece examines the evolving nature of these laws, shedding light on the challenges and complexities inherent in defining and combating human trafficking. The author's meticulous research and nuanced analysis reveal how shifts in legal frameworks may inadvertently dilute the effectiveness of anti-trafficking efforts. This article is a must-read for anyone interested in international law, human rights, and the ongoing fight against human trafficking. It serves as a vital resource for understanding the intricacies of legal responses to a global crisis. [Credit: American Journal of International Law]

The Continuing Struggle: Modern Slavery(the remaining referance is from the publication:Exploitation Creep and the Unmaking of Human Trafficking Law by the American Journal of International Law)

Today, an estimated 40.3 million people are trapped in modern forms of slavery. This encompasses forced labor, human trafficking, and debt bondage. In response, various measures have been implemented globally:

- **Legislation:** Laws like the U.K.'s Modern Slavery Act of 2015 aim to provide law enforcement agencies with the necessary tools to combat contemporary forms of slavery.

- **Awareness and Training:** Public awareness campaigns, along with training for law enforcement and legal professionals, play a crucial role in identifying and supporting victims.

- **Technological Innovations:** AI and other technologies are being harnessed to disrupt and prevent slavery practices, particularly in the realm of sex trafficking.

Despite these efforts, modern slavery remains a deeply entrenched issue, often exacerbated by contemporary policy decisions, particularly in the realm of immigration.

The Impact of Immigration Policies on Modern Slavery

Current immigration policies in countries like the U.S. and the U.K. inadvertently contribute to the perpetuation of modern slavery:

- **U.S. Immigration Policies:** Strict border controls and family separations have created conditions ripe for exploitation, making migrants vulnerable to trafficking and forced labor.

- **U.K. Immigration Laws:** Recent changes have made it increasingly difficult for victims of human trafficking to access support, leaving many without the necessary resources to escape their situations.

The Legal Framework Against Slavery

International law has established robust frameworks against slavery:

- **Vienna Convention on the Law of Treaties:** This established the jus cogens norm, recognizing slavery as a non-derogable offense.

- **Supplementary Convention on the Abolition of Slavery:** This broadens the definition of slavery, obligating states to abolish practices similar to slavery.

- **International Covenant on Civil and Political Rights:** Article 8 explicitly prohibits slavery, slave trade, and servitude.

However, the gap between legal frameworks and their implementation remains significant. For instance, the definition of slavery in the context of international human rights law and criminal law varies, leading to challenges in enforcement and victim support.

The Complexity of Modern Slavery

- **Characteristics of Modern Slavery:** The 1953 UN Secretariat report identifies six characteristics that give rise to slavery, including the treatment of individuals as objects of purchase and the absolute use of individuals for labor without compensation.

- **Trafficking in Persons Report:** This report highlights the extent of trafficking and the challenges in accurately estimating its prevalence due to factors like media skepticism and varying definitions.

- **Legal Challenges:** Cases like Tanedo vs. East Baton Rouge Parish School Board illustrate the complexities in legally addressing modern slavery under laws like the TVPA.

Bridging the Past and Present

The legacy of historical abolitionists and their relentless pursuit of freedom and equality serves as an enduring inspiration in the modern fight against slavery. While significant strides have been made through legislation, awareness campaigns, and technological advancements, challenges persist, particularly in the face of restrictive immigration policies and legal complexities.

To truly honor the work of past abolitionists, contemporary efforts must not only focus on eradicating slavery but also address the underlying systemic issues that perpetuate exploitation. This includes reforming immigration policies, ensuring robust legal frameworks, and maintaining vigilant public awareness. Only through a concerted and multifaceted approach can the vision of a world free from slavery, championed by figures like Truth, Tubman, Douglass, and Garrison, become a reality.

1. See, e.g., Walk Free, A World Without Slavery: I Believe in a World Where Everyone Can Walk Free, at

2. See, e.g., McGregor, Lorna, Applying the Definition of Torture to the Acts of Non-state Actors: the Case of Trafficking in Human Beings, 36 Hum. Rts. Q. 210 (2014) CrossRef Google Scholar.

3. See, e.g., Fahey, Diane L., Can Tax Policy Stop Human Trafficking?, 40 Geo. J. Int'l L. 345 (2009) Google Scholar.

4. See, e.g., Bravo, Karen E., Free Labor: A Labor Liberalization Solution to Modern Trafficking in Humans, 18 Transnat'l L. & Contemp. Probs. 545 (2009) Google Scholar.

5. See, e.g., Note, Remedying the Injustices of Human Trafficking Through Tort Law, 119 Harv. L. Rev. 2574 (2006).

6. See, e.g., Todres, Jonathan, Moving Upstream: the Merits of a Public Health Law Approach to Human Trafficking, 89 N. C. L. Rev. 447 (2011) Google Scholar.

7. See, e.g., Pope, James Gray, A Free Labor Approach to Human Trafficking, 158 U. Pa. L. Rev. 1849 (2010) Google Scholar; Shamir, Hila, A Labor Paradigm for Human Trafficking, 60 Ucla L. Rev. 76 (2012) Google Scholar.

8. See, e.g., Ethan B. Kapstein, The New Global Slave Trade, Foreign Aff., Nov.-Dec. 2006, at 103.

9. Luis CdeBaca, Ambassador-at-Large, Office to Monitor and Combat Traffick-

ing in Persons, Freedom Here & Now: Ending Modern Slavery, Remarks before the Women's Foundation of Minnesota and the Center for Integrative Leadership (May 8, 2012),

10. See Protocol to Prevent, Suppress and Punish Trafficking in Persons, Especially Women and Children, Supplementing the United Nations Convention Against Transnational Organized Crime, Art. 3, opened for signature Nov. 15, 2000, 2237 UNTS 319 [hereinafter UN Trafficking Protocol] (emphasis added).

11. See id.; Gallagher, Anne, Human Rights and the New UN Protocols on Trafficking and Migrant Smuggling: A Preliminary Analysis, 23 Hum. Rts. Q. 975, 984–86 (2001) CrossRef Google Scholar (discussing the debates over vague el-

ements of the definition, including, for example, "sexual exploitation").

12. The official interpretative notes to the UN Trafficking Protocol clarify that its use of the terms "exploitation of the prostitution of others and other forms of sexual exploitation" is "without prejudice to how States Parties address prostitution in their respective domestic laws." Report of the Ad Hoc Committee on the Elaboration of a Convention Against Transnational Organized Crime on the Work of Its First to Eleventh Sessions, Addendum, Interpretative Notes for the Official Records (Travaux Préparatoires) of the Negotiation of the United Nations Convention Against Transnational Organized Crime and the Protocols Thereto, para. 64, UN Doc. A/55/383/Add.1 (Nov. 3, 2000) (emphasis added).

13. U.S. Department of State, Trafficking in Persons Report 4 (2014) (letter from Secretary of State John Kerry, introducing the report). These reports all have the same title, distinguished by the change in the year of publication. For ease of citation, the short form for citing the reports will include the title prefaced by the year— for example, 2014 Trafficking in Persons Report.

14. See generally Denise Brennan, Life Interrupted: Trafficking Into Forced Labor in the United States (2013).

15. J. J. Gould, Slavery's Global Comeback, Atlantic (Dec. 19, 2012),

16. Otto, Diane, Remapping Crisis Through a Feminist Lens, in Feminist Perspectives on Contemporary International Law: Between Resistance and Compliance? 75

(SariKouvo, & Pearson, Zoe eds., 2011) Google Scholar.

17. Victims of Trafficking and Violence Protection Act of 2000, 22 U.S.C. §§7101–7110 (2000) [hereinafter TVPA], amended by Trafficking Victims Protection Reauthorization Act of 2003, 22 U.S.C. §§7101–7110 (Supp. III 2005), Trafficking Victims Protection Reauthorization Act of 2005, 22 U.S.C. §§7101–7110 (Supp. IV 2007), William Wilberforce Trafficking Victims Protection Reauthorization Act of 2008, 22 U.S.C. §§7101–7112 (Supp. III 2010), Trafficking Victims Protection Reauthorization Act of 2013, Pub. L. No. 113–4, 127 Stat. 136.

18. Chuang, Janie, The United States as Global Sheriff: Using Unilateral Sanc-

tions to Combat Human Trafficking, 27 Mich. J. Int'l L. 437, 449 (2006) Google Scholar.

19. Otto, Dianne, Lost in Translation: Re-scripting the Sex Subjects of International Human Rights Law, in International Law and Its Others 318, 324 (Orford, Anne ed., 2006) CrossRef Google Scholar.

20. Convention for the Suppression of the Traffic in Persons and of the Exploitation of the Prostitution of Others, opened for signature Mar. 21, 1950, 96 UNTS 271.

21. Anne T. Gallagher, The International Law of Human Trafficking 62 n.4 8 (2012); Gallagher, Anne T., Human Rights and Human Trafficking: Quagmire or Firm Ground? A Response to James Hathaway, 49 VA. J. Int'l L. 789,

790–93 (2009) Google Scholar.

22. Sassen, Saskia, Women's Burden: Counter-geographies of Globalization and the Feminization of Survival, 71 Nordic J. Int'l L. 255 (2002) CrossRef Google Scholar.

23. Mike Kay, the Migration-Trafficking Nexus: Combating Trafficking Through the Protection of Migrants' Human Rights (2003).

24. UN Trafficking Protocol, supra note 10.

25. UN Convention Against Transnational Organized Crime, Nov. 15, 2000, 2225 UNTS 209 (entered into force Sept. 29, 2003).

26. Gallagher, supra note 21, at 4.

27. The first draft of the protocol (by Ar-

gentina) limited its coverage to women and children. The United States advocated, instead, coverage of all persons "while recognizing that women and children [were] particularly vulnerable to trafficking." The protocol thus references "especially women and children" in its title and throughout its provisions. Ad Hoc Committee on the Elaboration of a Convention Against Transnational Organized Crime, Revised Draft Protocol to Prevent, Suppress and Punish Trafficking in Women and Children, Supplementing the United Nations Convention Against Transnational Organized Crime, at 1 n .1, UN Doc. A/AC.254/4/Add.3/Rev.1 (Feb. 22, 1999).

28. The work of the then UN Commission on Human Rights leading up to the Trafficking Protocol negotiations reveals no

discussion of how human rights standards apply to human trafficking. The UN General Assembly resolution encouraging states and regional economic organizations to sign and ratify the Organized Crime Convention and its protocols was framed exclusively in terms of crime control, with no mention of human rights concerns. See GA Res. 55/25 (Jan. 8, 2001).

29. UN Trafficking Protocol, supra note 10, pmbl. (noting the need to protect the victims' "internationally recognized human rights").

30. Gallagher, supra note 11, at 990–91.

31. UN Trafficking Protocol, supra note 10, Arts. 6, 7; see also id., Art. 9.

32. See Chuang, Janie A., Rescuing Traffick-

ing from Ideological Capture: Prostitution Reform and Anti-trafficking Law and Policy, 158 U. Pa. L. Rev. 1655 (2010) Google Scholar.

33. See, e.g., Farley, Melissa, Prostitution and Trafficking in Nine Countries: An Update on Violence and Posttraumatic Stress Disorder, 2 J. Trauma Practice 33 (2003) CrossRef Google Scholar; Kathleen Barry, The Prostitution of Sexuality (1995); Leidholdt, Dorchen, Prostitution: A Violation of Women's Human Rights, 1 Cardozo Women's L. J. 133 (1993) Google Scholar; MacKinnon, Catherine, Prostitution and Civil Rights, 1 Mich. J. Gender & L. 13, 28 (1993) Google Scholar. Sociologist Elizabeth Bernstein has labeled the feminist neo-abolitionist preference for punitive paradigms of justice as "carceral femi-

nism." Bernstein, Elizabeth, The Sexual Politics of "New Abolitionism," 18 Differences 128 (2007) CrossRef Google Scholar.

34. Chuang, supra note 33, at 1669. For incisive analyses of these feminist moves, see Halley, Janet, Kotiswaran, Prabha, Shamir, Hila & Thomas, Chantal, From the International to the Local in Feminist Legal Responses to Rape, Prostitution/Sex Work, and Sex Trafficking: Four Studies in Contemporary Governance Feminism, 29 Harv. J. L. & Gender 335 (2010) Google Scholar.

35. See The Sex Sector: the Economic and Social Bases of Prostitution in Southeast Asia (Lin Lean Lim ed., 1998); Raymond, Janice G., Legitimating Prostitution as Sex Work: UN Labour Organiza-

tion (ILO) Calls for Recognition of the Sex Industry, Coalition Against Trafficking in Women (July 12, 1999),

36. The ILO submitted brief, narrowly focused written comments on the protocol but was absent from the coalition of other international organizations—including the Office of the High Commissioner for Human Rights, UN High Commissioner for Refugees, UNICEF, and the International Organization for Migration—that actively provided input during the protocol negotiations. See Ad Hoc Committee on the Elaboration of a Convention Against Transnational Organized Crime, Note by the International Labour Organization on the Additional Legal Instrument Against Trafficking in Women and Children, UN Doc.A/AC.254/CRP.14 (June 16, 1999).

37. See, e.g., UN Office on Drugs and Crime, Model Law Against Trafficking in Persons, UN Sales No. E.09.V.11 (2009),

38. See, e.g., UN Office on Drugs and Crime, Issue Paper: Abuse of a Position of Vulnerability and Other "Means" Within the Definition of Trafficking in Persons (2012).

39. UN Convention Against Transnational Organized Crime, supra note 25, Art. 32(1); Gallagher, supra note 21, at 460–61 (discussing the Conference of Parties' decision to extend its monitoring, information exchange, cooperation, and other functions to the Trafficking Protocol).

40. Chuang, supra note 18, at 454–56. These sanctions are neither humanitarian- nor trade-related and include withdrawal of

both U.S. direct financial assistance and U.S. support for multilateral aid packages. 22 U.S.C. §§7106(a), 7107(d)(1). Countries receiving the lowest ranking (Tier 3) in the annual TIP Report have a ninety-day grace period during which to improve their performance before the sanctions determination is made. The U .S. president can waive sanctions if necessary to protect U.S. national interests, promote the goals of the TVPA, or avoid significant adverse effects on vulnerable populations. Id., §7107(d).

41. 22 U.S.C. §7106(b)(1). The four minimum standards, in summary form, are as follows:

The government should prohibit and punish acts of severe forms of trafficking in persons.

42. Chuang, supra note 18, at 464–65; Gal-

lagher, Anne T. & Chuang, Janie, The Use of Indicators to Measure Government Responses to Human Trafficking, in Governance by Indicators: Global Power Through Quantification and Rankings 327 (Davis, Kevin E., Fisher, Angelina, Kingsbury, Benedict & Merry, Sally Engle eds., 2012) Google Scholar. Thailand paid a reported U.S.$400,000 to a prominent lobbying firm to (unsuccessfully) persuade the United States not to downgrade Thailand to Tier 3 in the 2014 Trafficking in Persons Report, supra note 13, at 58. Felicity Lawrence & Kate Hodal, Thai Government Condemned in Annual U.S. Human Trafficking Report, Guardian (June 20, 2014), .

43. See National Security Presidential Directive/NSPD-22, at 2 (Dec. 16, 2002), at (noting that U.S. anti-trafficking policy

"is based on an abolitionist approach to trafficking" and that the United States "opposes prostitution... as contributing to the [trafficking] phenomenon"). The "model law" distributed to states to help them comply with the "U.S. minimum standards" included a trafficking definition that explicitly encompassed noncoerced prostitution, inaccurately citing the UN Trafficking Protocol for authoritative support. U.S. Department of State, Office to Monitor and Combat Trafficking in Persons, Legal Building Blocks to Combat Trafficking in Persons §§100, 206(a) (2004).

44. For in-depth discussion of these measures, see Chuang, supra note 33, at 1680–94. The "anti-prostitution pledge" was struck down as unconstitutional in the HIV/AIDS funding context. USAID

v. Alliance for Open Soc'y Int'l, 133 S.Ct. 2321 (2013).

45. International Labour Office, A Global Alliance Against Forced Labour: Global Report Under the Follow-Up to the ILO Declaration on the Fundamental Principles and Rights of Work 14 (2005).

46. See, e.g., Convention Concerning the Prohibition and Immediate Action for the Elimination of the Worst Forms of Child Labour, opened for signature June 17, 1999, 2133 UNTS 161 (entered into force Nov. 19, 2000); Convention Concerning the Abolition of Forced Labour, opened for signature June 25, 1957, 320 UNTS 291 (entered into force Jan. 17, 1959); Convention Concerning Forced or Compulsory Labour, opened for signature June 28, 1930, 39 UNTS 55 (en-

tered into force May 1, 1932).

1. U.S. Department of State, Trafficking in Persons Report 6 (2006) (noting that the 2006 report focuses on "slave labor and sexual slavery").

2. See, e.g., U.S. Department of State, Trafficking in Persons Report 17 (2009) (debt bondage among migrant laborers), 18 (involuntary domestic servitude), 26 (strengthening prohibitions against forced labor and fraudulent recruitment of foreign workers).

3. See, e.g., id. at 5, 13, 21, 22 (using the term "forced prostitution"); U.S. Department of State, Trafficking in Persons Report 8 (2010) (stating that "[p]rostitution by willing adults is not human trafficking regardless of whether it is legalized, de-

criminalized, or criminalized").

4. U.S. Department of State, Fact Sheet: The Link Between Prostitution and Sex Trafficking (Nov. 24, 2004)

5. U.S. Department of State, What Is Trafficking in Persons? (June 2014), at

6. See International Labour Organization, Buried in Bricks: A Rapid Assessment of Bonded Labour in Afghan Brick Kilns 6 (2011), adf (describing intergenerational transference of debt among bonded laborers in the Afghan brick-making industry).

7. See Beate Andrees & Mariska N.J. van der Linden, Designing Trafficking Research from a Labour Market Perspective: The ILO Experience, Int'l Migration, Jan. 2005, at 55, 64 (explaining

that non-trafficked forced laborers exercise more agency in exiting forced labor than trafficked ones).

8. 2006 Trafficking in Persons Report, *supra* note 53, at 6, 10; U.S. Department of State, Trafficking in Persons Report 6 (2007); U.S. Department of State, Trafficking in Persons Report 7 (2008); 2009 Trafficking in Persons Report, *supra* note 54, at 8; 2010 Trafficking in Persons Report, *supra* note 55, at 7.

1. This position has been communicated to the author by TIP Office personnel, including Ambassador CdeBaca on multiple occasions, and confirmed by both TIP Office and Department of Labor personnel as the source of much debate within the U.S. government.

2. U.S. Department of State, Human Rights Reports, at http://www.state.gov/j/drl/rls/hrrpt/. For example, ILAB had viewed intergenerational bonded labor as within its portfolio and outside that of the TIP Office. Interview with International Labor Affairs Bureau, Department of Labor, in Washington, D.C. (Dec. 2012).

3. Close collaboration with states, NGOs, trade unions, companies, and international organizations is required to develop strategies to promote internationally recognized workers' rights and to address the loopholes in labor frameworks that facilitate forced labor. Interview with International Labor Affairs Bureau, supra note 65.

4. DRL's analysis of states' anti-trafficking efforts tended to be more nu-

anced and targeted at structural factors. See Human Rights Reports, supra note 65; Chuang, supra note 18, at 476, 481–83 (discussing, as examples, Cuba and Venezuela).

5. Bureau of International Labor Affairs, U.S. Department of Labor, International Child Labor and Forced Labor Report. For example, ILAB found that Brazil had made "significant advancement" (the highest level) in 2012 in eliminating the worst forms of child labor, whereas the TIP Office found that Brazil had made only a middling effort (Tier 2) in combating trafficking (including child labor). U.S. Department of State, Trafficking in Persons Report 103 (2013).

6. The ILO's 2011 draft survey guidelines for estimating forced labor, entitled Hard

to See, Harder to Count, offered both "narrow" and "broad" definitions of trafficking. Whereas the "narrow" version retained the trafficked versus non-trafficked distinction, the "broad" definition noted that "[i]rrespective of movement ... any adult or child worker engaged in forced labour is classified also as a victim of human trafficking." International Labour Office, Hard to See, Harder to Count: Survey Guidelines to Estimate Forced Labour of Adults and Children 20 (2011),).

7. International Labour Office, ILO Global Estimate of Forced Labour 13 (2012). Tellingly, chapter 1 of a 2014 ILO report on the profits of forced labor is entitled "Measuring Forced Labour, Human Trafficking and Slavery: Why Definitions Matter." Rather than offering

an interpretation of the trafficking definition, however, the discussion notes only that, except for trafficking for organ removal, "trafficking" is covered by the ILO Forced Labour Convention. International Labour Organization, Profits and Poverty: The Economics of Forced Labour 3–4 (2014).

8. U.S. Department of State, Trafficking in Persons Report 45 (2012). Closer review reveals the ILO's implicit adherence to the trafficked/non-trafficked distinction regarding forced labor, despite avoiding the term "trafficking." In Hard to See, Harder to Count, supra note 69, at 19, the ILO states that while movement is not necessary to prosecute a case of human trafficking, "national policy-makers may nonetheless decide to distinguish between 'trafficked' and 'non-trafficked' (or

other forms of) forced labour... to devise differentiated policy responses that are best adapted to the national context and specific target groups." Applying this distinction, the 2012 Global Estimate assesses "how many people end up being trapped in forced labour following migration" (9.1 million, or 44% of the total) versus those who are "subjected to forced labour in their place of origin or residence" (11.8 million, or 56% of the total). International Labour Organization, ILO 2012 Global Estimate of Forced Labour: Executive Summary (2012), at [3]. See also Profits and Poverty: The Economics of Forced Labour, supra note 70, at 8 (offering the same analysis).

9. The protocol was adopted June 11, 2014.

10. See Tripartite Meeting of Experts on

Forced Labour and Trafficking for Labour Exploitation, Report for Discussion at the Tripartite Meeting of Experts Concerning the Possible Adoption of an ILO Instrument to Supplement the Forced Labour Convention, 1930 (No. 29), para. 144 (2013) (noting as discussion point number 1 whether and how to define the relationship between forced labor and trafficking); International Labour Standards Department and Programme on Promoting the Declaration on Fundamental Principles and Rights at Work, Report and Conclusions of the Tripartite Meeting of Experts on Forced Labour and Trafficking for Labour Exploitation, app., para. 2, ILO Doc. GB.317/INS/INF/3 (2013) (implying a distinction between trafficking and forced labor, but leaving its precise contours unaddressed).

11. See International Labour Conference, Protocol to Convention 29 (June 11, 2014); International Labour Conference, Text of the Recommendation on Supplementary Measures for the Effective Suppression of Forced Labour (June 11, 2014).

.

12. See generally Kolben, Kevin, Labor Rights as Human Rights, 50 VA. J. Int'l L. 449 (2010) Google Scholar (contrasting the approaches of labor rights and human rights to social change, and assessing the turn to human rights discourse by labor scholars and labor organizations).

13. See, e.g., Shamir, supra note 7, at 107. This critique echoes the trenchant internal critiques of the human rights system made by Makau Mutua and David

Kennedy. See, e.g., Mutua, Makau, Savages, Victims, and Saviors: the Metaphor of Human Rights, 42 Harv. Int'l L. J. 201 Google Scholar; Kennedy, David, The International Human Rights Movement: Part of the Problem?, 15 Harv. Hum. Rts. J. 101, 118 (2002) Google Scholar. For a response to Shamir's critique, see Todres, Jonathan, Human Rights, Labor, and the Prevention of Human Trafficking: A Response to a Labor Paradigm for Human Trafficking, 60 Ucla. L. Rev. Discourse 142, 158 (2013) Google Scholar.

14. Interview with Confidential Source no. 1 (labor advocate), in Washington, D.C. (May 28, 2013) (noting that framing projects as related to trafficking significantly increased their funding possibilities).

15. See Kolben, supra note 76. The ILO's

adoption of its 1988 Declaration on Fundamental Principles and Rights at Work has been invoked (and criticized) as an example of this turn toward a human rights approach. International Labour Conference, ILO Declaration on Fundamental Principles and Rights at Work and Its Follow-Up (June 18, 1998), a the annex was revised June 15, 2010); See Alston, Phillip & Heenan, James, Shrinking the International Labor Code: An Unintended Consequence of the 1998 ILO Declaration on Fundamental Principles and Rights at Work, 34 N.Y.U. J. Int'l L. & Pol. 101 (2004) Google Scholar. The declaration was partly an attempt to revitalize an "ineffective and weak" ILO. Helfer, Laurence R., Understanding Change in International Organizations: Globalization and Innovation in the ILO, 59 V and. L. Rev. 649, 704 (2006) Google Scholar.

The advent of the modern anti-trafficking regime prompted the ILO to pursue eradication of forced labor—one of the four "core" labor standards under the declaration—with renewed vigor. The ILO Governing Body created a Special Action Programme to Combat Forced Labor (SAP-FL) in 2001 to spearhead its work on forced labor and trafficking.

Christian?- Forward(Bonus Read)

E very person's life is a profound mystery. Deep and invisible currents make us who we are, and the world around us is full of secret purposes and laws. One reaction to all this mystery is to treat it as a problem to be solved, and to do everything possible to be informed and in control. But another way is to bow down in ignorance and confess our limitations. Religion and spirituality, for eons, has been closely connected and offered creative ways to become individuals of depth and compassion by embracing spirituality.

The religions have a cherished cargo, but they often fail in their job by moralizing, intellectualizing, and defending themselves to such an extent that their real intention is clouded. Today, individuals all over the world are deserting the religions in disgust and anger. Still, everybody has an instinct for transcendence. Individuals know that some kind of spiritual life is essential, and so a lot of people are exploring on their own or joining new churches and communities. They differentiate between their own personal spirituality they've found and the religious institution they've abandoned.

THE ARGUMENT—IS THERE A GOD?

The philosophy of religion is one of the most captivating areas of philosophy. It addresses not only the repeated question, "Is there a God?" but also the questions, "If there is, then what is He like?" The most important question of all is, "What does that mean for us?"

These are questions that everyone should ask themselves at some point. This book attempts to demystify the philosophy of religion and help people to reach answers and form their own views on these questions.

"Is there a God? Or is just being spiritual enough?"

Is There a God?

The debate concerning God's existence has, naturally, been a question most have asked since anyone can remember. That doesn't mean that no progress has been made. Some of the classic arguments for God's existence have been largely deserted, others have been refined, and new arguments regularly appear.

The search for an answer to the question of God's existence shouldn't be written off as futile merely because the question is an old one.

"If there's a God, then what is He like?"

If they're successful, then none of the classic arguments for God's existence proves exactly the same thing. One argument, for example, aims to prove the existence of a perfect being. Another argument aims to prove the existence of a Creator concerned with humanity. Each of these arguments bears not only on the question of God's existence but also on the question of His nature.

What is Christian Spirituality :

Christian spirituality is a journey marked by transformation and pursuit of the sacred, characterized by a profound interplay between the divine and the human. It is the voyage from the old self to a new creation, as epitomized in 2 Corinthians 5:17. This explanation will explore the depths of this transformative journey, examining the scriptural foundations, the historical context, and the personal experiences that define spirituality from a Christian perspective. This inquiry will dissect the metaphysical implications of Christian beliefs and practices, aiming to illuminate the intricate tapestry that is the Christian spiritual quest.

In the Christian narrative, the journey begins with an acknowledgment of one's separation from the divine due to sin, as depicted in the story of the Fall in Genesis. The subsequent narrative arc of the Bible can be seen as humanity's quest to bridge this chasm, culminating in the life, death, and resurrection of Jesus Christ. According to Christian doctrine, it is through Christ that salvation and reconciliation with God are made possible, as John 3:16 poignantly summarizes the promise of eternal life for all who believe.

This salvation promise is the cornerstone of Christian spirituality, which is not a mere adherence to doctrine but an experiential walk with God. It involves a daily renewal, a continuous effort to live in accordance with the teachings of Christ. Romans 12:1-2 exhorts believers to present their bodies as a living sacrifice and to not conform to the world but be transformed by the renewing of their minds.

This transformation is both an instantaneous state of being "in Christ" and a progressive sanctification.

Christian spirituality is inherently communal and historical, rooted in the tradition of the Church. It is not a solitary or abstract concept but a lived reality shaped by the collective experience of believers throughout the ages. The practices of worship, sacraments, prayer, and community life are the means by which individuals participate in this shared spiritual journey. The church fathers, mystics, and reformers have all contributed to the rich tapestry of Christian spirituality, each adding their understanding and experiences of the divine.

The personal dimension of Christian spirituality is equally critical. It is where the transcendent truths of the faith become intimately interwoven with the fabric of one's life. The Psalms reflect a range of human emotions, from despair to joy, and illustrate a personal and honest relationship with God. The spirituality of the Psalms is not one of escape from reality but an integration of one's entire being with the divine narrative.

Moreover, Christian spirituality involves a mission—it is outward-looking and service-oriented. Following Christ's example, believers are called to serve others, as evidenced by the Great Commission in Matthew 28:19-20 and the parable of the Good Samaritan in Luke 10:25-37. Spirituality thus encompasses social justice, care for the poor, and the reconciliation of relationships, reflecting the kingdom values that Jesus preached.

In the modern era, the challenge for Christian spirituality is to maintain its authenticity and transformative power in a world that often seems at odds with spiritual values. It is to live out the Beatitudes in a contemporary context, embodying the principles of the Sermon on the Mount in a society characterized by individualism and materialism.

Christian spirituality is also marked by a future hope—the eschatological dimension that looks forward to the ultimate fulfillment of God's kingdom. The book of Revelation paints a picture of a new heaven and a new earth, where God will dwell with his people. This hope shapes the present reality of believers, infusing their journey with purpose and direction.

In conclusion, Christian spirituality is a multifaceted journey that involves a profound transformation from an old way of being to a new life in Christ. It is grounded in the scriptural narrative, expressed through the historical and communal life of the Church, experienced personally in the depths of one's being, manifested in service to others, and oriented towards the future hope of God's kingdom. The essence of this spirituality is captured

> in the Apostle Paul's declaration in Galatians 2:20: "I have been crucified with Christ and I no longer live, but Christ lives in me. The life I now live in the body, I live by faith in the Son of God, who loved me and gave himself for me." This verse not only encapsulates the essence of Christian spirituality but also invites individuals to embark on the most profound journey one can undertake—the journey towards enlightenment and salvation, led by faith in Jesus Christ.

Christian Spirituality places an individual on the highest pedestal in life, aligning closely with the teachings of Jesus. Its goal, as reiterated in the Bible, is attaining salvation. This path is not about what we desire or want; it is about living life as it was meant to be, according to God's will. Those who earnestly seek this path of Spirituality are often able to manifest destiny by aligning their will with God's. This is beautifully reflected in Galatians 5:22-23, which speaks of the fruit of the Spirit - love, joy, peace, forbearance, kindness, goodness, faithfulness, gentleness, and self-control.

Many individuals, even with materialistic goals, unknowingly tread the path of Christian Spirituality and find success. This is not by chance but through the divine law. Christian Spirituality means that before we ask God for material blessings, we should aim to give back to the community, embodying Christ's teachings of love and service.

Christian Spirituality certainly aids in mastering one's destiny. As believers progress on this path, they develop a positive outlook towards life, echoing Romans 8:38-39, "For I am convinced that neither death nor life, neither angels nor demons, neither the present nor the future, nor any powers, neither height nor depth, nor anything else in all creation, will be able to separate us from the love of God that is in Christ Jesus our Lord." This scripture assures believers of God's unending love and support, guiding them towards fulfilling their divine destiny.

Christian Spirituality transforms a negative thinker into a person of faith and hope. In this field, there is no room for negativity, as faith in Christ instills a sense of purpose and direction. This path reassures us that there is something greater than our mere existence - a relationship with God. It is this relationship, as promised in John 14:16-17, that guides us on the right path through the Holy Spirit, the Spirit of truth who lives within us.

Christian Spirituality is universal, transcending different religions, dogmas, or creeds. It brings people together, making the world seem like one large family under God. In this spiritual domain, the wanton desires of the flesh cease to exist, as one is led by the Spirit.

Christian Spirituality is the essence of life, cleansing us of all impurities and guiding us towards true value and purpose. It is not merely about being religious; it is about living out the core values taught by Christ. It is through this Spirituality that God guides humanity towards its destined goal.

The practice of Christian Spirituality is not confined to theory or sacred texts alone. It is a living, breathing practice that should permeate every aspect of our lives. As believers, we aim to reach the end of our cosmic life with salvation, a gift made possible through faith in Jesus Christ. As 1 Corinthians 10:13 reminds us, "No temptation has overtaken you except what is common to mankind. And God is faithful; he will not let you be tempted beyond what you can bear." This scripture reinforces the grace and faithfulness of God in our spiritual journey.

Why not practice this pure, Christian Spirituality all the time, embracing the love, guidance, and salvation offered through our faith in Jesus Christ?

Christian Spirituality

More than ever, in these tumultuous times, it's crucial to discern truth from deception, a task made clearer through the lens of devout Christian faith. This chapter aims to illuminate the distinction and symbiosis between religion and spirituality from a conservative Christian viewpoint.

In this era of confusion and chaos, clarity emerges through the Christian faith. Commonly, there is confusion between being merely religious and being genuinely spiritual. It is a misconception that all religious individuals are inherently spiritual. Equally erroneous is the belief that a God-fearing individual is incapable of wrongdoing. Scripture tells us, "for all have sinned and fall short of the glory of God" (Romans 3:23).

Christianity teaches that life is inherently spiritual. This spirituality is rooted in a relationship with Christ. As stated in 2 Corinthians 5:17, "Therefore, if anyone is in Christ, the new creation has come: The old has gone, the new is here!" This passage underscores that true spirituality is found in transformation through Christ.

The level of one's spiritual awareness is not a matter of race, status, or creed, but a matter of the heart and soul, transformed by Christ's love. "There is neither Jew nor Gentile, neither slave nor free, nor is there male and female, for you are all one in Christ Jesus" (Galatians 3:28). This unity in Christ transcends all earthly divisions.

Not everyone recognizes this spiritual truth. Many are distracted by worldly concerns - stress, materialism, negative attitudes - which cloud their spiritual perception. These barriers hinder a deep relationship with God, as emphasized in Romans 12:2, "Do not conform to the pattern of this world, but be transformed by the renewing of your mind."

Turning away from organized religion is not the solution; rather, the answer lies in a deeper understanding of one's faith. Christianity advocates for a personal relationship with God, guided by Scripture and the Holy Spirit. This relationship is not bound by external appearances or rituals, as stated in 1 Samuel 16:7, "The Lord does not look at the things people look at. People look at the outward appearance, but the Lord looks at the heart."

Christianity calls for spreading love, joy, and peace, mirroring the fruits of the Spirit described in Galatians 5:22-23. The Christian faith empowers individuals to think freely, guided by the wisdom of the Holy Spirit and the teachings of Christ.

Christian spirituality is not a pursuit of aggressive piety but a state of being in Christ. It's about conscious living in alignment with God's will, as stated in Proverbs 19:21, "Many are the plans in a person's heart, but it is the Lord's purpose that prevails."

The contrast between religion and spirituality, from a Christian perspective, is stark. Religion, wrongly practiced, can lead to division and legalism. In contrast, true Christian spirituality brings unity, peace, and a focus on Christ's love and redemption.

In these changing times, Christians are called to awaken to the spiritual realities described in Scripture. As Ephesians 6:12 states, "For our struggle is not against flesh and blood, but against the rulers, against the authorities, against the powers of this dark world and against the spiritual forces of evil in the heavenly realms." Recognizing this spiritual battle is crucial for a Christian's journey.

The path forward is to embrace the goodness found in Christ, spreading His love and joy. As Romans 12:21 instructs, "Do not be overcome by evil, but overcome evil with good." This is the Christian's mission - to be a light in a dark world, spreading the hope and love of Christ to allIn these challenging times, it is more important than ever for Christians to stand firm in their faith, anchoring themselves in the truth of the Gospel and the promises of God. This chapter continues to explore the principles of devout Christian living in a world filled with confusion and chaos.

The Christian call is to be vigilant and discerning, recognizing the spiritual realities that shape our world. As we navigate these turbulent times, it is the teachings of Christ that provide clarity and direction. The Bible in Ephesians 6:12 reminds us of the spiritual battle that underlies our earthly struggles, urging us to put on the full armor of God so that we can take our stand against the devil's schemes.

Christians are called to be agents of change, embodying the virtues of Christ in their daily lives. This means actively choosing to spread love, peace, and hope, even in the face of adversity. As Romans 12:21 teaches, "Do not be overcome by evil, but overcome evil with good." This is the essence of Christian spirituality - to be a beacon of light in a dark world, showcasing the transformative power of Christ's love.

In a world that is rapidly evolving, with new challenges and paradigms emerging, Christians are called to remain steadfast in their faith. They must be like the wise man who built his house on the rock, unshaken by the storms of life (Matthew 7:24-27). This firm foundation in Christ enables believers to navigate the complexities of modern life with wisdom and discernment.

Christians are encouraged to engage with the world, not as passive bystanders but as active participants in God's redemptive plan. They are to be salt and light (Matthew 5:13-16), preserving goodness and illuminating truth in a world that often seems lost in moral and spiritual confusion

As society grapples with various moral and ethical dilemmas, the Christian perspective remains grounded in the teachings of Scripture. Christians are called to uphold biblical values, advocating for truth, justice, and righteousness. This involves being a voice for the voiceless, defending the weak and marginalized, and promoting a culture of life and dignity for all, as reflected in Proverbs 31:8-9.

Christians understand that true spirituality is not merely a private affair but has public implications. It compels them to engage with societal issues, bringing the wisdom of God's Word to bear on contemporary challenges. By doing so, they demonstrate the relevance and transformative power of the Gospel in every area of life.

Finally, amidst the trials and tribulations of this world, Christians hold onto the hope of eternity. They are comforted by the promise in Revelation 21:4, "He will wipe every tear from their eyes. There will be no more death or mourning or crying or pain, for the old order of things has passed away." This eternal perspective shapes their response to the present, infusing their lives with purpose and meaning, and empowering them to face the future with confidence and hope.

In conclusion, the Christian approach to spirituality is deeply rooted in the truth of Scripture, the teachings of Christ, and the power of the Holy Spirit. It is a spirituality that transcends the challenges of the present age, offering hope, redemption, and transformation both now and for eternity.

CHriSTiaN AFFirMaTiONS

Continuing from the conservative Christian perspective, the use of imagery, poetic expression, and affirmations must consistently direct believers towards a deeper understanding and living out of biblical principles. This approach recognizes the centrality of Scripture in shaping a believer's life and worldview.

In the context of conservative Christian theology, the use of imagery, poetic expression, and affirmations must be deeply rooted in Scripture and align with sound doctrine. This approach understands that faith is not merely a mixture of knowledge and ignorance but a firm belief in God's truth as revealed in the Bible.

In a conservative Christian view, imagery and poetic expression serve as tools to convey the deep truths of Scripture, not as ends in themselves. Stories and parables, as Jesus often used, are valuable for teaching, reproof, correction, and training in righteousness (2 Timothy 3:16). They are not merely for pleasure or to ponder unresolved issues but to guide believers in God's truth. The use of imagery must lead to the solidification of faith, rooted in the certainty of God's Word, as depicted in Jeremiah 29:11, which assures us of God's plans for our welfare and hope.

The emotional insecurities often ascribed to personal failures or upbringing are, in this viewpoint, more accurately understood as spiritual voids that only a relationship with Christ can fill. As Ephesians 6:12 states, our struggle is not merely against flesh and blood but against spiritual forces. Therefore, a spiritual position based on Christian faith is essential for true security and stability.

Affirmations, in a devout Christian context, are not mere positive statements but are to be grounded in biblical truth. They are not tools to foster spiritual emptiness but to affirm God's promises and truths in one's life. Christians are encouraged to be discerning when reading religious texts, always testing what they read against Scripture, as warned in 2 Timothy 4:3, regarding the danger of accumulating teachings that merely suit personal desires.

Christian affirmations should reflect a deep understanding of God's nature and His works. For example, affirming God's providence in providing for needs, as seen in the Lord's Prayer (Matthew 6:11), is more aligned with conservative Christian beliefs than affirmations focusing solely on material wealth or personal satisfaction.

A conservative Christian approach to daily affirmations would focus more on spiritual growth and God's kingdom. For instance:

- "Lord, help me to seek first Your kingdom and Your righteousness" (Matthew 6:33).

- "I am fearfully and wonderfully made in the image of God" (Psalm 139:14).

- "I trust in the Lord with all my heart and lean not on my own understanding" (Proverbs 3:5).

- "I am a new creation in Christ; the old has gone, the new is here" (2 Corinthians 5:17).

- "God has not given me a spirit of fear, but of power, love, and a sound mind" (2 Timothy 1:7).

- "I can do all things through Christ who strengthens me" (Philippians 4:13).

- "I am an ambassador for Christ" (2 Corinthians 5:20).

To summarize from a conservative Christian perspective, faith is deeply intertwined with a sound understanding of Scripture. Imagery, poetic expressions, and affirmations are valued only when they align with biblical truth and lead believers to a deeper relationship with God, understanding His will and purpose for their lives as revealed in His Word. In conservative Christianity, living a life that reflects the teachings of Scripture is paramount. This means not only understanding the Bible intellectually but also embodying its truths in daily life. As Luke 1:28,38 highlights Mary's submission to God's will, believers are encouraged to similarly embrace God's plans for their lives, even when they may not fully understand them. This surrender is not born out of ignorance but out of trust in God's sovereignty and goodness.

The focus is not just on personal spiritual growth but also on impacting the world for Christ. Believers are called to be witnesses to the truth of the Gospel, living out their faith in such a way that it draws others to Christ. As Matthew 5:16 says, "Let your light shine before others, that they may see your good deeds and glorify your Father in heaven."

A key aspect of conservative Christian philosophy is the vigilance against false teachings and doctrines that deviate from biblical truth. 2 Timothy 4:3 warns of a time when people will turn away from sound doctrine. In response, believers are encouraged to be discerning, grounded in the Word, and led by the Holy Spirit to recognize and reject teachings that contradict the Bible.

This vigilance extends to the realm of spiritual practice. While affirmations can be helpful, they must be based on and consistent with biblical teachings. The focus of affirmations should be on God's attributes, promises, and the transformation He brings, rather than material gains or self-centered desires.

Conservative Christian theology emphasizes the importance of viewing all aspects of life through the lens of Scripture. This includes understanding one's identity, purpose, and daily living in light of biblical teachings. Jeremiah 29:11, for instance, is often quoted to affirm God's plans for hope and a future, encouraging believers to trust in God's sovereign plan for their lives.

In conclusion, from an ultra-devout, right-leaning conservative Christian perspective, faith is not a blend of knowledge and ignorance, but a confident trust in the revealed Word of God. Imagery and poetic expression are used to deepen understanding and appreciation of biblical truths. Affirmations are rooted in Scripture, reinforcing a biblical worldview and guiding believers in their walk with Christ. This approach to spirituality is marked by a steadfast adherence to the Bible, a commitment to living out its teachings, and a focus on sharing the transformative power of the Gospel with the world.

pain and suffering

Best

Sellers
The Chronicles of Mary
Magdelene Series

Mary's Salvation
The Illuminated Path
Jerusalem's Faith
Paul's Odyssey
Andrew's Adventures
Mary's Celestial Journey
In the Company
of Angels
John's Journey
Heaven's Warriors
Isabella's Divine Destiny

Steve Taylor
Https://maryschronicles.online